Past Masters
General Editor Keith Thomas

Bach

Past Masters

AQUINAS Anthony Kenny
ARISTOTLE Jonathan Barnes
FRANCIS BACON Anthony
  Quinton
BACH Denis Arnold
BAYLE Elisabeth Labrousse
BERKELEY J. O. Urmson
THE BUDDHA Michael Carrithers
BURKE C. B. Macpherson
CARLYLE A. L. Le Quesne
CLAUSEWITZ Michael Howard
COBBETT Raymond Williams
COLERIDGE Richard Holmes
CONFUCIUS Raymond Dawson
DANTE George Holmes
DARWIN Jonathan Howard
DIDEROT Peter France
GEORGE ELIOT Rosemary Ashton
ENGELS Terrell Carver

GALILEO Stillman Drake
HEGEL Peter Singer
HOMER Jasper Griffin
HUME A. J. Ayer
JESUS Humphrey Carpenter
KANT Roger Scruton
LEIBNIZ G. MacDonald Ross
LOCKE John Dunn
MACHIAVELLI Quentin Skinner
MARX Peter Singer
MONTAIGNE Peter Burke
THOMAS MORE Anthony Kenny
WILLIAM MORRIS Peter Stansky
MUHAMMAD Michael Cook
NEWMAN Owen Chadwick
PASCAL Alban Krailsheimer
PLATO R. M. Hare
PROUST Derwent May
TOLSTOY Henry Gifford

Forthcoming

AUGUSTINE Henry Chadwick
BERGSON Leszek Kolakowski
JOSEPH BUTLER R. G. Frey
CERVANTES P. E. Russell
CHAUCER George Kane
COPERNICUS Owen Gingerich
DESCARTES Tom Sorell
DISRAELI John Vincent
ERASMUS James McConica
GIBBON J. W. Burrow
GODWIN Alan Ryan
GOETHE T. J. Reed
HERZEN Aileen Kelly
JEFFERSON Jack P. Greene
JOHNSON Pat Rogers
KIERKEGAARD Patrick Gardiner
LAMARCK L. J. Jordanova

LEONARDO E. H. Gombrich
LINNAEUS W. T. Stearn
MENDEL Vitezslav Orel
MILL William Thomas
NEWTON P. M. Rattansi
PETRARCH Nicholas Mann
ROUSSEAU Robert Wokler
RUSKIN George P. Landow
RUSSELL John G. Slater
ST PAUL G. B. Caird
SHAKESPEARE Germaine Greer
ADAM SMITH D. D. Raphael
SOCRATES Bernard Williams
SPINOZA Roger Scrutton
VICO Peter Burke
VIRGIL Jasper Griffin
and others

Denis Arnold

Bach

Oxford   New York

OXFORD UNIVERSITY PRESS

1984

*To my friends of the
Nottingham Bach Choir*

Oxford University Press, Walton Street, Oxford OX2 6DP

London Glasgow New York Toronto
Delhi Bombay Calcutta Madras Karachi
Kuala Lumpur- Singapore Hong Kong Tokyo
Nairobi Dar es Salaam Cape Town
Melbourne Auckland

and associated companies in
Beirut Berlin Ibadan Mexico City Nicosia

Oxford is a trade mark of Oxford University Press

British Library Cataloguing in Publication Data

Arnold, Denis
Bach.—(Past masters)
1. Bach, Johann Sebastian
I. Title II. Series
780'.92'4 ML410.B1
ISBN 0-19-287555-8
ISBN 0-19-287554-X Pbk

Library of Congress Cataloging in Publication Data

Arnold, Denis.
Bach.
(Past masters)
Bibliography: p.
Includes index.
1. Bach, Johann Sebastian, 1685-1750. 2. Composers—Germany—
Biography. I. Title. II. Series.
ML410.B1A96 1984 780'.92'4 [B] 83-15141
ISBN 0-19-287555-8
ISBN 0-19-287554-X (pbk.)

Set by Colset Private Limited
Printed in Great Britain by
Cox & Wyman Ltd, Reading

Preface

Most Past Masters have communicated their ideas in words. Bach communicated his in sound. This does not make him less a master, but it does pose difficulties for a commentator writing in prose. There have been many attempts to prove that music is a language. That it is a means of communication is scarcely deniable; that it functions in the way of a normal language is much more open to doubt. Primarily this is because it has little symbolism closely connected with objects or actions. It is possible to convey a sigh by making a singer breathe before and/or after the word (or, as in Italian, by breaking up the word sos-pi-ro); and there is a kind of realism in 'painting' the scourging of Christ by relatively loud, sudden chords, as in Bach's *St Matthew Passion*. Such symbols are few and to expand their range by analogy is fraught with problems. We commonly talk about scales going 'upward' or 'downward' but some composers have managed to set that most potent of images in the Mass 'Et ascendit in caelum' with a 'downward' motif; others have surprisingly ignored the visual concept completely and written a series of chords moving neither 'up' nor 'down'. Thus for a writer on music to paraphrase sound in words is to move from one to another, unlike medium.

It used to be held that music is essentially about emotional expression. Thus words must be sought to convey the emotions evoked by the composer, in the manner of those *belles-lettres* paraphrases which were not uncommon in the late nineteenth-century writers and critics. This will not do. The composer composes because words will not satisfy his desire for order. His means can be described by technical words; 'he modulates into the sub-dominant' or 'he extends the four bar pattern into a five bar phrase' – this is the kind of language favoured by the musicologist. Indeed, the modern musicologist often uses diagrams of varying visual complexity to show the composer's patterns which would otherwise be conveyed only by over-complicated syntax.

For these reasons, the musicologist nowadays rarely attempts a prose paraphrase of a composition, less still of a body of compositions. He usually makes a detailed technical analysis of a piece, which he may compare with analyses of other pieces. He is looking for the conventions of the music: whether it uses a few keys or many, strongly repeated rhythmic patterns or relatively weak but flowing melody, whether the orchestration is brilliant or restrained. Then he sees how the composer diverges from those conventions. It was sometimes held that there was a generalised 'style of the age' which each composer adapted to his own individual use. Today, that is doubted; and indeed if each composer has a core of 'finger prints' (as the late Ernest Newman called them) it is also true that his own conventions change as he lives and works. Each work embodies its own procedures and the analysis will reveal the difference between what is established convention and what is unusual within the piece. In fact, music is not so much the expression of emotion as the patterning of ideas. Composers talk in terms of problems: is it possible to write a piece which will sound satisfactory using only a single melodic strand (as in Bach's music for solo violin or cello); or can one invent a fugue subject which can be used in continual stretto? One composer of this writer's knowledge set himself the problem of writing Passion Music using specifically twentieth-century operatic techniques to avoid any reference to the past. This is no way to emotional self indulgence, or to follow simple inspiration.

The composer, then, thinks in terms of technical devices.

To explain Bach, a technician above all other technicians, to the general reader who has a limited knowledge of musical terminology, I have therefore written what might be called a 'musical biography'. This gives the facts about Bach's life with extensive discussions of the music which interested him at any time and the ways he reacted to it. Since the works I refer to are usually easily available on gramophone records, it should not be too difficult for the reader without knowledge of musical notation at least to find out the sound which was important to Bach and, with a little perseverance, to sense his approach to formal patterns. This approach has the advantage that it not only refers to what we know best (i.e. his music) but gives a proper sense of proportion to his life: for wine and women have always come a long way after song in a great composer's consciousness.

The suggestions for further reading represent in no way a bibliography. If such is needed, it may be found in the article 'Bach' in *The New Grove*, where it will be seen to consist mainly of articles in specialist journals, usually in German. It would be dishonest of the present author to pretend that he had read it all or even most of it. Nevertheless, he hopes that he has charted a clear path through its thickets.

Acknowledgements

Quotations from H. T. David and A. Mendel (eds.), *The Bach Reader*, © 1945, 1966 W. W. Norton & Co., Inc., are included by kind permission of W. W. Norton & Co., Inc. The passage from D. R. Hofstadter, *Gödel, Escher, Bach: an Eternal Golden Braid* (1979), on p. 75, is included by kind permission of The Harvester Press, and of Basic Books, Inc.

Contents

1 Origins *1*

2 *Kapellmeister* at Cöthen *17*

3 Leipzig *36*

4 The legacy *87*

Further reading *99*

Index *101*

1 Origins

The Bach family represents the most formidable example of a musical dynasty. Musicians are often the children of musician-parents: Mozart, Beethoven and Brahms are only those at the front of the mind. Is it Nurture or Nature that makes this relationship? For Mozart, surely nature. The process of Wolfgang's musical development was too rapid for it to be the product even of the finest teaching. But the Bach dynasty is another matter. There were musician-Bachs in the sixteenth century: the last of the line died in 1846. In between, there was no generation without a musician. They were all related: and even using quite strict criteria, seventy-five of them made their living, or part of it, by practising music. Nurture or Nature? The latter, one is tempted to say again, for surely it must be a gift which spreads itself so widely, over so many generations. A closer examination of the careers of the Bachs teaches otherwise. For, of these seventy-five, one was a genius, half a dozen others men of fame and distinctive talent. The others are, for the most part, not even the *Kleinmeistern* so beloved of German music historians. They were members (often violinists) of the 'town music'; organists at churches, sometimes the most important of their town, but by no means always; at best they became *Kantors*. They were the 'locals' of Thuringia: rarely did they travel abroad, even to study in the fashionable music centres of Italy or France. They learned their trade at home, taught by father or uncle or their colleagues. This surely is Nurture.

The matter is important. The one genius of the Bach family, Johann Sebastian, himself had no doubts 'I had to work hard. Anyone who works as hard as I did, will get as far',

1

he is reputed to have said to his pupils. And although there is no untruer remark in the history of music, this stern attitude of the Protestant Work Ethic is at the heart of much of his music. Especially in his later years was he very much a Bach.

As indeed he was at his inauspicious beginning. He was born at Eisenach on 21 March, 1685, son of Johann Ambrosius, court trumpeter and director of the town musicians; who, in turn, was son of Christoph, town musician at Arnstadt in the mid-seventeenth century. He was sent to the local grammar school (Latinschule) when he was about six; and his musical education, no doubt arranged by his father, apparently did not at first include the playing of keyboard instruments. Both Johann Sebastian Bach's parents died before he was ten, and he was then brought up by his elder brother, then in his mid-twenties and organist at the small town of Ohrdruf. It was there that he began to practise the organ and, although his brother was no composer, he taught him the principles of composition, largely by copying out the music of older organists – Froberger, Kerll, Pachelbel. There was also school to attend, another grammar school, the Lyceum, which had a wide curriculum and at which he did well.

By 1700, there were problems about studying in Ohrdruf. Johann Sebastian's brother's family was growing and there was little room in his house. So one of the masters at the Lyceum found him a place at the Michael School (for poor boys) at Lüneburg in northern Germany. Johann Sebastian paid, as it were, for his tuition by singing treble in the 'Matins' choir, the inner group of the church choir. Thus, at the age of fifteen he achieved financial independence, which state he owed to music. Whatever his later inclinations (and one feels that he would sometimes have preferred another *métier*) it was to continue thus for the rest of his life. At school, he studied a wide range of subjects, including some science and also German poetry; but it seems likely that it was at this time, his later teens, that he began to blossom musically. At the Johanneskirche, the organist, Georg Böhm, was very distinguished and Bach certainly came to know him. The young man also took the trouble to visit Hamburg at least twice (a journey of thirty miles each way on foot), once to hear the most famous organist of the North German school, J. A. Reincken, then at the Catharinenkirche. And what an instrument he had to play! Bach remembered it many years later, the splendour of its reeds and the power and evenness of the thirty-two-foot Principal and the pedal Trombone stops. These are signs that the organ was becoming the centre of his interests. Also significant is his visit to Celle, the court of a Frenchified nobleman who had an orchestra modelled on that of Versailles – and indeed including many French players. Since French music was all the rage in many parts of Europe, this must also have opened a horizon for a young musician so far acquainted more with the circumscribed ways of Thuringian church music.

The next step was obvious. Bach applied for the job of organist at the Jacobikirche at Sangerhausen, not far from Halle, in 1702 and would have obtained it but for the intervention of the Duke of Weissenfels, who had his own favoured candidate. It seems likely that the Duke felt some sense of obligation towards Bach and secured him some work at the court at Weimar. While he was there, he advised on the building of a new organ at Arnstadt in the Bonifaciuskirche, and the church elders were so impressed that in August 1703 they offered him the post of organist. It was reasonably well paid – certainly for a man of eighteen – and the duties were not very heavy. So Bach began his career as a church organist.

The word 'organist' needs a little stressing. Bach was not the *Informator choristarum* or *Kapellmeister*. Certainly the Neukirche (as the rebuilt St Bonifacius was now called) occasionally put on cantatas – but that was not Bach's job, as he insisted, when the elders were inclined, a year later, to put pressure on him to perform them. He was organist – playing preludes etc., and accompanying the hymns; and there is ample evidence that he never really relished the job of directing a choir. No doubt it was too imperfect an instrument for him, since organ playing tends to encourage a type of perfection of co-ordination, a neatness beyond the capacity of ensembles of ordinary musicians. And that the organ was still his primary interest is indicated by his next trip. He went to Lübeck to hear Buxtehude. This was a mammoth excursion, a matter of at least 250 miles each way. He obtained a month's leave of absence from the church fathers, but it was not nearly enough, and he was hauled over the coals when he returned. No matter, he had heard the great organist – and had probably heard some of the *Abendmusiken* for which the church at Lübeck was famous, and which eventually was to lead to the elaboration of the church cantatas of Bach's later years. Did he come back home with ideas too great for little Arnstadt? There was in fact a first-class row with the authorities: Bach was providing too elaborate accompaniments to the hymns (he was probably adding flourishes or even miniature cadenzas at the ends of lines); he was not getting on well with the choir boys and students; he was still unwilling to compose and direct cantatas; he had even invited a girl to sing in the church (probably his cousin and future wife). The row died down, but the desire to move must have become strong. His reputation was increasing and when a job at the more important church of St Blasius at Mühlhausen became vacant, it was an obvious step forward. In June 1707 he was offered and accepted the post of organist there with a salary equal in money to that of Arnstadt to which various 'perks' were added – fuel and bushels of grain.

It is at Mühlhausen that Bach the composer appears.

Before this we know little of him. No doubt he had composed some preludes based on hymn tunes, as well as harmonisations of the tunes themselves; and if some of the so-called '18' chorale preludes of a later autograph album do date back to Arnstadt, one can see why the church elders complained of over-elaboration, for they reveal the virtuoso organist inside the young man – the heir of Buxtehude and Böhm. But the first firmly datable compositions of any stature were the cantatas for Mühlhausen: the famous Easter piece *Christ lag in Todesbanden*, the festive work for the inauguration of the town council *Gott ist mein König*, and funeral piece *Gottes Zeit ist die allerbeste Zeit* and a wedding cantata for one of his wife's aunts *Der Herr denket an uns*. All were occasional pieces, it may be noted, and no deepening feeling for the Lutheran church should be read into them. *Gott ist mein König* is indeed the first of his works to use the brilliant sonorities of the 'town music' with its three trumpets and drums, the oboes, bassoons and flutes, and although the autograph title page has at its head what was to become familiar on Bach's manuscripts 'Jesu Juva' (Jesus help me), it is in fact a 'state motet', in a tradition dating back to the Renaissance, especially in Germany. The exception to the purely 'ceremonial' type cantata is the well known *Christ lag in Todesbanden*, an elaboration of a chorale, its several verses being set as duets, trios and solos with choruses and a brief overture for the modest instrumental ensemble of five-part strings (the two independent lines for violas darken the sound). Here Luther's evocation of Christ's agony and death are matched in Bach's music by his emphasis on the semitone which begins the chorale tune and which seems to become an 'emblem of death' (the German scholar Schering's epithet for it); and this emblem may be held to foreshadow Bach's later inclinations, although again it is inadvisable to read too much of Bach's own beliefs into it, for this kind of elementary symbolism is no more than many Baroque composers would have used, though certainly with less skill and consistency. It came naturally to the organist, whose daily bread came from accompanying hymn singing.

Nevertheless it was probably not his compositions which were responsible for his rising reputation, for there is evidence that the congregation (and maybe the pastor) at St Blasius were not too happy about such elaborate church music. His playing, on the other hand, had certainly brought him pupils and had also attracted the notice of the Duke of Weimar who offered him the post of organist at his court in the early summer of 1708. Bach had been at Mühlhausen for only a short time and had been treated well by the church council. But he had married and his wife was pregnant, so he tendered his resignation on 25 June; the elders accepted it with the proviso that he should continue to supervise the various improvements to the organ already in hand.

The money was better at Weimar; it became even better with time for he was much appreciated by his employer. He needed it, for six children were born to him in his Weimar years, between 1708 and 1715 though two, a set of twins, died shortly after their birth in 1713. Quite apart from such material circumstances, it was a happy time for Bach. He had no responsibilities, at least at first, for choirs and ensemble music; he was the organist, with time to practise and compose for his instrument. He was allowed to make alterations to the castle organ, his builder being an old acquaintance. A friend and distant relative, J. G. Walther (who later became known for one of the earliest music lexicons) was organist at the Stadtkirche. Bach was sought out by a succession of pupils and two of his children, Carl Philipp Emanuel (b. 1714) and Wilhelm Friedmann (b. 1710) were to become very distinguished musicians.

The result can be felt in the organ music of those years,

especially in the large scale works called Fantasia or Toccata or Prelude usually culminating in a Fugue. It is these pieces which provide the basis of the organist's repertoire to this day, and the reason for this is that they were written by a master player. Most of them stem from that tradition of improvisation which was central to the church organist's art, as he filled musical gaps in the ceremonial, prepared for the entries or departures of priest, high priest or monarch and expressed the mystery of the Host. Moreover it was a tradition especially practised in Germany for centuries, even before the Reformation, as pieces marked Preludium can be found in such 'Gothic' organ books as the famous one from Buxheim or the late Renaissance tablature books of the German organist and publisher Schmidt.

The art of composing such pieces is to allow the fingers to invent something relatively elementary and natural: there is no time to think of intricate patterns. The opening must be arresting – a brilliant scale passage or loud chords patterned in distinctive rhythms. Then (and this is the difficult part) to develop these simple ideas, to allow them to suggest subsidiary themes, to allow them to roam from key to key, to introduce new concepts (for instance a slow section in between fast, virtuosic movements) yet always to feel that the first ideas are in the background. It is an art perhaps best revealed by Bach not in his organ works but in the toccatas for harpsichord written probably in these Weimar years. In these, superficial flourishes can later become intricate accompaniment figures, a simple scale a lively gigue. As for the fugues which are so often the culmination of these frozen written-down improvisations, they seem also to have themes that come from the fingers rather than the mind. The 'Wedge' which expands each way from a single note; the doodling with thumb and first two fingers in the splendid D major (BWV 532); the alternation of thumb and little finger in the most famous of all, the D minor (no doubt derived from the cross bowing of a violin theme); these are not the hallmarks of a great contrapuntist but of a young, energetic player. Only later does the mind take over and the themes are thoroughly worked out; even then, they bring glory on the player, especially when the working out involves the pedals. For one of the most admired features of Bach's playing in his lifetime was his footwork. To listen to the finger-bound theme of the D major in full cry and fully exposed on the pedals, foot over foot, is to relish Bach's virtuosity, his triumph of physical co-ordination. Organists have to be neat men: their mistakes do not, like a doctor's, quietly die, but are all too obvious and blatant, especially on powerful instruments. Bach, having heard Buxtehude's twinkling feet, tests this skill to the utmost. Yet one can well imagine that he improvised these fugues, for the material is so finger- and foot-worthy. Much of it is exuberant, the work of a still-young man, glorying in his physical powers, and the brilliant sound of the organ.

Moreover, he was still capable of learning new tricks. About 1713, his prince and some Weimar musicians seem to have brought back some of the latest fashionable music from the Netherlands where a publisher had got hold of concertos by young Vivaldi (only six or seven years older than Bach) of Venice, twelve of which came out as Op. 3 with the title *L'Estro armonico*. This too is exuberant music, though of a different kind; and it is not difficult to see why Bach was attracted by it. Vivaldi, as virtuoso a violinist as Bach was an organist, reorganised the concerto from the model provided by the non-virtuoso Corelli, so as to allow it to show off his prowess. His concertos had three well-defined movements, the outer two fast, the middle one slow. The slow movement was in effect an operatic aria, the violin taking the place of the theatrical diva. Usually this is an emotional piece, the climax of a scene, and one which encourages the display of beautiful tone. The first movement of the concerto is often highly extended, marked by easily memorable, strongly rhythmic themes announced in a ritornello which opens and closes the movement and also (in shortened versions) punctuates the rest of the movement, while the soloist provides his embellishments in the episodes in between. The relationship between orchestra and solo, between themes and episodes, can be quite sophisticated, especially because Vivaldi had grasped the principle of key modulation, that is that the home key, or tonic, represents a resting place, while other keys give varying degrees of discomfort or tension. Thus (and this must have been the attraction for Bach who had been working in a more restricted medium) there is the possibility of contrasting emotions – and perhaps even more significantly, pastel shades of those emotions. The final movement was more often a simpler piece built from dance rhythms and less virtuosic in attitude.

Vivaldi's music swept Europe in the two decades from 1710, driving out the older Corellian concerto grosso (except in far-flung places such as England), and encouraging a new generation of violin virtuosi – Locatelli, Geminiani, Veracini – who took to touring abroad and came to dominate such courts as that at Dresden where Italian musicians ruled the roost for many years. Perhaps encouraged by his own prince, Bach, having no violinists of the virtuosity of these Italians to hand, transcribed some of these concertos for keyboard (his friend at the Stadtkirche, J. G. Walther did the same for other modern Italians such as Albinoni) and, in his way, added a few things here and there, to remove any suspicion of simplicity. But, more importantly, thereafter Vivaldi's ritornello structure permeates his music in all kinds of media – not just music for organ, or orchestra; cantatas and even the 'Gloria' for the *B minor Mass* use its techniques.

Bach had good reason to want to please his prince at this

time for he was hoping for promotion; and (although commentators anxious to protect his good name interpret the documents otherwise) it looks as though he used an invitation to become organist at the Liebfrauenkirche in Halle as a lever to become *Konzertmeister* at Weimar in 1714. His duties were now enlarged. He had to direct the orchestra and also he had to write a cantata each month for the court chapel, a requirement which over the next three years resulted in at least thirty-three works. These were to be rather different from those written for the Blasiuskirche, not surprisingly since the court chapel was not an ordinary Protestant church controlled by a council of elders, but the personal chapel of the Duke; and the Duke's tastes in vocal music may be seen in a piece which Bach probably wrote in 1713, for the birthday of a friend of his employer, Duke Christian of Saxe-Weissenfels. It is a 'hunting cantata' (it is called a 'cantata di caccia' on the manuscript title page) although it would have been called a 'serenata' or something similar in Italy, where the genre arose. Such works were the successors of those operas which in the early seventeenth century had been produced to celebrate a royal birthday or marriage. Opera, alas, was now too complicated and too expensive, certainly for a minor member of the nobility. Instead, a musical entertainment in the manner of opera, but requiring little or no scenery, few rehearsals (since it did not need to be learned by heart) – and perhaps less virtuoso singers – was found agreeable. Which is precisely what this 'hunting cantata' *Was mir behagt* consists of. The libretto was written by Salomo Franck, then secretary to the Weimar court, where his duties included looking after the ducal library and his own coin collection (an interest at times giving rise to an apt image in his libretti). Franck was a poet of no great distinction, but he had written a series of texts for religious cantatas as early as 1694 and in 1711 published a book of verse, *Geist-und weltliche Poesie*. His 'hunting cantata' is in effect a double dialogue between Diana and Endymion, and Pan and Pales. The pastoral setting was much in tune with early eighteenth-century tastes (this was the time of those open air fêtes at Versailles), while the hunting scenes were certainly suitable for lusty German noblemen. Franck provided a text divided into recitatives and arias with a couple of choruses or ensembles (in Italian opera at this time 'coro' means simply the solo singers all joining in), the one at the end a typical homage to the duke.

To this rather conventional conception, Bach surprisingly brings real imagination: surprisingly because this was not the usual *métier* for a Lutheran organist, although Italian opera composers (such as Agostino Steffani at Hanover who had produced a similar piece *La lotta d'Hercole con Acheloo* in 1689) would have been quite at home in it. Bach can have had little knowledge of opera, since he had never lived in a centre where it was regularly given – as, for example, Hamburg where Handel had learned his trade. Especially he can have had no experience in composing recitative. Moreover, the operatic aria style had to be broader, more obvious and popular than anything he had written for the organ. The first sign of his appreciation of the new needs comes in his orchestration, with its delicious use of *corni da caccia* (hunting horns), recorders and *oboe da caccia*. The pastoral and hunting images were, no doubt, obvious – but that was exactly what the occasion needed. Similarly, the aria style is lighter, more direct than one might have expected from the learned organist: it is no wonder that one of the arias has become so well known in the English speaking world as 'Sheep may safely graze'. It can indeed be only the general view that Bach was really a religious composer that prevents the more frequent performance of the whole of the piece, with its final gigue-like aria for Pan and that over a ground bass for Pales (while the woolly sheep are merrily driven through two widely praised meadows, long live this Saxon hero).

So the Duke of Weimar could have good hopes of his monthly cantatas. In the event, Bach's surviving cantatas which can be ascribed to his Weimar years show both a youthful exuberance and a talent for adapting all kinds of pre-existing forms to his needs. The resources at his disposal were a little strange. He had a small group of good instrumentalists: a quartet of string players (perhaps one or two more); a skilled bassoonist and, seemingly, some good oboists at times; and he could call on the military for trumpets and drums for festive occasions. His 'choir' hardly merits the word. He had two each of sopranos, altos, tenors and basses, the sopranos being probably falsettists (they are called 'discantista' in the chapel lists); but if the group was small, each member was probably very competent. There was also a group of half a dozen boy soloists, although how skilled they were is open to question. It was the reverse of Mülhausen where cantatas were based on a good choir and ordinary soloists. Here the soloists were good and the choir meagre. This goes a good way to explain his adoption of the new style cantata.

The other salient fact was, of course, the proximity of Salomo Franck and his cantata texts. Some English commentators have wondered how Bach could set these extravagant, overweening verses. Germans, on the other hand, are generally kinder, probably because they accept the Baroque conventions more easily, whereby the poetaster deliberately pushes to the edge of taste in sentiment and image. In any case, Bach set about fifteen of them and some of these are among the best of his pre-Leipzig cantatas. Franck provided for a cantata a poem divided into perhaps ten sections, each intended to be set as either recitative or aria. The operatic analogy at once comes to mind, but it is the difference between opera and this kind of cantata that seems more important. In opera, the singer expresses his thoughts and tells the audience what has happened in the recitative, before expressing his emotions in the aria. But in the cantata there is usually no story to tell and feeling and thinking substantially overlap. So recitative seems rather superfluous, which explains why Bach often uses a full orchestral accompaniment rather than simply the dry chords of harpsichord and organ. This recitative also becomes a vehicle (and a very succinct one) for emotion, differing from aria in that words are not repeated, changes of mood can be achieved quickly and phrase structures are more irregular. Another difference is that in opera it is usually the same singer who goes from recitative to aria; in the cantata, there is no necessity for this, so frequently one singer will sing the recitative, another the aria, if the differing emotions of the two make this desirable. Another occasional difference comes from the fact that Franck sometimes writes a dialogue section, a meeting between Jesus and the Soul of the Believer (for example as in Cantata 152 *Tritt auf die Glaubensbahn*). Strange though it seems today, dialogue ensembles were very rare in eighteenth-century opera seria, for the reason that they must perforce present simultaneously differing emotions for the two characters, and the librettists of opera seria preferred to display only one 'pure' emotion at a time. In church music, on the other hand, ensemble music has always been popular, partly because the singers are rarely capable of virtuoso feats expected in operas, partly because the emotional emphasis should be on mankind in general rather than the individual. So it came naturally to have dialogue pieces. The other kind of ensemble which was frequently used in opera, the closing piece where all the characters come down to the front of the stage to ring down the curtain, as it were, also finds a place, for Bach frequently adds a hymn at the end of a cantata otherwise for soloists, sometimes harmonising it simply, sometimes providing a more elaborate setting with instrumental accompaniment (as in Cantata 147, *Herz und Mund und That und Leben*, where the final movement is the chorale setting known in English as 'Jesu joy of man's desiring').

These cantatas, then, have some of the trappings of opera rather than being truly operatic; and in other ways Bach manages to disguise the theatrical origins of the genre. One way comes in his imaginative use of instruments. True, there are occasional operatic memories; this time in his use of the form and manner of the French overture as an opening movement, developed by Lully for theatrical entertainments at Versailles. Yet in the main, Bach remembers that he has only a chamber ensemble at his disposal. This has an advantage: all the players, especially the string players, are skilled. They can play intimate expressive music, which is what the introductory sinfonias tend to be; and they can play virtuoso obligato parts in the arias. Here Bach's natural pleasure in elaboration is seen. He was never a man for keeping things simple: later in life, when copying out what had become one of the most famous pieces of religious music, Pergolesi's *Stabat Mater*, he could not forbear to add an independent viola part, in place of the composer's simple part doubling the bass, as was customary in the eighteenth century. Here, at Weimar, he used violin or oboe to provide a counter melody to the voice, so that the textures should not become too simple. One suspects that it was as a result of combining voice and instrument that Bach's melodies became more complicated, encrusted with decoration, than those of many of his contemporaries.

The other trait which appears somewhat surprisingly in a hitherto predominantly instrumental composer is Bach's penchant for word painting, for in these Weimar cantatas, the texts are often conveyed most vividly. A great deal has been written about this aspect of Bach's work, with some, notably Albert Schweitzer in his great book on Bach published in 1905, maintaining that Bach used a complicated system of musical motifs to express every image and mood of his cantata texts. And it is true that German theorists of the time advocated a theory of the 'affections', whereby various figures represented the emotional meaning of the text. There can be little doubt that Bach was acquainted with such ideas, much more doubt about his

2 *Kapellmeister* at Cöthen

Surprise has sometimes been expressed that Bach should have been blown off course, in accepting this post at a Calvinist court where church music was of little importance. But this is to see Bach, as the nineteenth-century commentators liked to see him, the Protestant *Kantor*, devout and devoted to his Church. A more rational view is to see this as the natural progression of the musician from the narrow confines of the organ loft towards the head of his profession. That would have been to take charge of music at Dresden or Berlin; in the meantime, Cöthen was well paid, a decently equipped court from the musician's point of view, and, more than that it had a sympathetic prince. This prince, who was only 24, had managed to persuade his mother to set up an orchestra during his regency, had done the Grand Tour, and studied music in Rome. He had picked up some musicians when the Berlin court orchestra had been disbanded in 1713/14, and by 1716 had a *Kapelle* of eighteen musicians. He paid Bach 400 thalers a year, to which were added various other fees, like the rent for a rehearsal room in Bach's home. There was a good Lutheran school for Bach's children, a matter which must now have been assuming some importance, since Wilhelm Friedmann was now seven and Carl Philipp Emanuel three (both went to this Lutheran school in due course, Bach clearly preferring it to the longer established Calvinist school). Bach soon found a house to rent, and must have been content that his master was so sympathetic to music.

The routine of the court cannot have been very different from that at Weimar. The main difference must surely have lain in the fact that Bach was now in charge of the whole

Kapelle and could arrange its rehearsals to suit himself. The monthly cantata was now not necessary. Bach did have to compose the occasional cantata, for the name-day or birthday of his employer (indeed he dashed away from Weimar as soon as he was let out of prison on 2 December in 1717 so as to produce music for the prince's birthday on the tenth). We do not possess the work then performed, nor later ones for similar occasions with the exception of one, *Durchlauchtster Leopold* (BWV 173a), perhaps composed shortly after Bach had left Cöthen. But this can scarcely be regarded as typical, the text a homage piece of no great artistic merit, the music a succession of recitatives and arias for soprano and bass, with a final chorus (or rather ensemble). This is simpler music than many of the Weimar cantatas, with dance rhythms as the basis for several of the numbers, such as the bourrée in the soprano aria 'So schau dies holden Tages' and the polonaise in the final chorus, while the duet 'unter seinem Pur, pursamm' actually has the instructions 'al tempo di minuetto' written in the score. There were other cantatas, a few for church, a few for New Year celebrations: but if the simpler style of *Durchlauchtster Leopold* is anything to go by, Bach's style had been changing for the more modern, the more obviously comprehensible.

Which is to say it was influenced by the instrumental genres of the time; dance music was popular, albeit not always lacking in sophistication. But when he first arrived at Cöthen, he must have been glad that he had had the experience of transcribing Vivaldi's concertos in the period around 1713, after his former employer's return from Holland; for here was modern orchestral music suitable for his band. Whether (like the orchestras in eighteenth-century England) Bach sent away for the parts of Vivaldi's Op. 3 (well known to him), Op. 4 called *La stravaganza*, or the two books of *Concerti a 5 stromenti* published in 1716–17, or whether he had a manuscript source of supply (as they seem to have had at the Dresden court) we do not know. What is certain is that he composed his own Vivaldian-type concertos in some profusion. The Brandenburg Concertos are indeed his nearest equivalent to a Vivaldi set of six concertos; while the violin concertos in A minor and E major, and the marvellous double concerto for violins in D minor are believed to belong to his Cöthen years. In addition there are a number of harpsichord concertos, later played at Leipzig, which clearly represent arrangements of earlier works for different combinations which may well have started life then.

All these are Vivaldi-like in general attitudes – though considerably unlike in stylistic detail. They are usually works in three movements (the first Brandenburg Concerto is very much the odd one out, and with its peculiar orchestration seems to belong to an early period and place – perhaps Weimar pre-1713 or Weissenfels with its *corni da caccia*); and when in the third Brandenburg Concerto there are only two, it is evident that a slow movement is missing, perhaps originally improvised by leader or harpsichordist (who would have been Bach himself at the first performance). Also like Vivaldi are the themes, with their motor rhythms reinforced by internal repetitions (the first movement of the third Brandenburg is the archetype), their clear outlines (the 'hammer blows' of the E major violin concerto's first three notes are a well known example), and the ample ritornello forms which govern not only the first movements but also the finales, which can be very extended. The aria-like nature of the slow movements is equally derived from Vivaldi, the sheer beauty of those of the E major concerto or the D minor concerto for two violins surely owing much to the example of the Italian. And there are those moments of virtuosity, the rapid passage work for the violin in the last movement of the fourth Brandenburg Concerto or the impossibilities of the trumpet part in the second.

But the fact that these are 'moments' rather than complete concertos underlines the differences between Italian virtuoso and German *Kapellmeister*. The fact is that Vivaldi's use of cross string writing for violin often sounds much harder than it is; while Bach's extended lines often sound much easier than they are. The virtuosity of the trumpet is necessary to play the simple sounding tunes of the second Brandenburg Concerto and a mistake sounds like a mistake rather than a desperate attempt to do something very difficult. Similarly in the third Brandenburg Concerto the fact that there is no single soloist or solo group obscures the fact that all the parts have their difficulties – it is a true 'concerto for orchestra'. For Bach 'concerto' does not imply difficulty (he was one of those men for whom everything came too easily for the concept to have much meaning) but 'a concerted piece' in which ensemble and co-ordination was the underlying challenge.

This is made plain also by the nature of the individual lines, in which he shows the old penchant for counterpoint. Whereas Vivaldi after announcing his themes breaks them up, Bach enjoys the extension of ideas. It is the paragraph which is the unit, not the sentence, still less the clause. The examples are countless: the openings of the first movement of the fourth Brandenburg Concerto, and the finale of the D minor violin concerto, the jolly but extended tune of the last movement of the second Brandenburg, fashioned for the limited notes that the natural trumpet can play yet going on and on as if it were only for violin and flute. Best of all, this spinning out of a melodic line can be seen in the slow movements, especially of the violin concertos, the most famous of which, that in E major, shows Bach's power, not so much of ornament as of natural embellishment, for to try to find an 'archetype' free of ornament is meaningless, so deeply are the decorative figures embedded in the violin line. The most beautiful example of all is probably the slow movement of the double violin concerto, for here the spinning and weaving of the thread go hand in hand. Bach writes it in the manner of a trio sonata, two melody instruments accompanied lightly by the bass and 'harmony instruments' (harpsichord) to fill in the middle. He selects the long bar in twelve/eight time beloved of the Italians since it minimises the number of accents to favour the flow (which is why it was such a favourite with Bellini a century later, for it is the essence of *bel canto*). Then he writes a lengthy paragraph for one violin, imitating it immediately with the other. Thereafter they join, and as in the best conversations, one will introduce an idea, the other take it up and alter it slightly to lead it back to the first one – and so it goes on. The thread is stretched, yet the weave gives a feeling of strength and depth. Whereas with Vivaldi's similar movements (and Bach certainly knew a quite similar piece in the D minor concerto of his Op. 3) one can whistle or hum the tune, Bach's is too complex: it lingers in the mind rather than throat and remains endlessly fascinating, the more so since the harmony is also made complex by the dissonances (though not very severe) inherent in the ornamentation in both the violin parts.

Another very un-Vivaldian trait is the orchestration of the Brandenburg Concertos. Truly, Vivaldi does use varied combinations of instruments, including wind (especially for the Dresden court with which he established links in the 1720s and 30s) but he rarely seems to fashion his material out of the instruments' natures and sonorities as does Bach. Leaving aside the first concerto of the set as indeed extraordinary, none of the rest use a recognisably ordinary tone colour. The second, for trumpet, violin, recorder and oboe is absolutely without precedent. The third, which might seem almost normal in requiring strings alone, confounds expectation by dividing each section – violins, violas and cellos – into three. The fourth is perhaps best described as a violin concerto (though its solo instrument is in fact a 'violino piccolo', not the ordinary fiddle); but in that case why are there two 'Flauti in echo' which dominate the slow movement? The fifth is perhaps by similar reasoning a harpsichord concerto (in which case it is one of the earliest of the genre) especially since the cembalo has a mighty written-out cadenza in the first movement. But the parts for flute and 'violino principale', if less virtuoso in their demands, are little less important. The sixth is an 'orchestral' concerto, but the scoring for two viole da gamba (by this time an obsolescent instrument although Bach's orchestra included a virtuoso on it, C. F. Abel) as the uppermost parts to contend with violas and cellos of the violin family might belong to the sixteenth century rather than the eighteenth. Every choice shows a sense of refinement in the sphere of sonorities, which could be found curious in a man who was quite capable of rearranging his compositions to suit differing circumstances; but one should never mistake a practical musician for one who does not have a keen ear; and it is noticeable that when he does rewrite he rarely leaves alone, rather does he tend to consider the conception anew and re-compose to make it sound totally natural.

Presumably Bach had all the instruments necessary to perform these concertos at Cöthen: even for the first, he may have had the horn players on a visit from Weissenfels. Nevertheless, we may wonder whether the Duke of Brandenburg had these eccentric ensembles at his disposal. Admittedly he had asked Bach, when the composer had been in Berlin searching for a new harpsichord for his employer, for some compositions; but did he expect anything like this? Was Bach expecting a decent *pourboire* for the set, as the elegance of the title page of his presentation copy seems to suggest?

> Six Concerts
> Avec plusieurs Instruments
> Dediées

A Son Altesse Royalle

Monseigneur

CRETIEN LOUIS

Marggraf de Brandenbourg etc: etc: etc:

par

Son tres-humble & tres obeissant Serviteur

Jean Sebastian Bach

Maitre de Chapelle de S.A.S: le

Prince regnant d'Anhalt-Coethen.

Was he perhaps expecting a subsidy for its publication, for publishers liked sets of six or twelve concerti? In either case, Bach was disappointed. No donation seems to have been sent from the royal coffers, nor did Bach join the popular Italians in the lists of European music publishers. Not a note appeared in the lists of Etienne Roger of Amsterdam, still less Walsh of London. Which, considering the contents, was not surprising.

The French of the title page and the dedication reminds us that not only was that language the lingua franca of the German nobility: it was also the musical language or rather style of much of their preferred music. Bach's other compositions for Cöthen reflect this taste. As well as Vivaldian concertos, Bach wrote several French suites or 'ouvertures' as they were often called. They can hardly be described as 'Lullian', since although that composer had inaugurated the taste for such music, he had been dead some thirty-four years by the time Bach took up the genre, and Bach was no conscious antiquarian. He followed the outline of the Lullian pattern, namely a pompous, dotted, slow, opening movement, followed by a fugal section (not usually learned or even very skilful in French hands), which was in turn followed by a group of dances. Then, as always, he changed the manner of it. Of the two orchestral suites which were probably written at Cöthen, the one in C major (known as No. 1 today) is a comparatively modest affair for oboes, bassoon and strings, resources which might indeed have been in use in France; and the dances are French in pattern. Yet Bach's usual complexity of texture and its resulting weight made it quite unlike anything by the French. The lightness of tread which keeps the dances feeling as though they were still suitable to accompany physical activity tends to disappear. This is, paradoxically, less true of the D major suite (No. 4 in modern numeration), for although Bach here added trumpets and drums to woodwind and strings, the very simplicity of melody which they insisted upon meant that the tunes have greater clarity, while the brass's penchant for sharp articulation helps rhythms to be projected firmly. This is surely openair music (the sound is reminiscent of Handel's D major suite of the *Water music* or the *Music for the Royal Fireworks*, both of which were for the great outdoors) and very invigorating it is. It is not, however, particularly French.

The major results of the popularity of French dances in fact are to be found in Bach's music for the clavier (the term can mean in this context either harpsichord or clavichord). It is surprising that during the Weimar years he seemingly composed little of this, his keyboard energies going almost exclusively into organ music. Now, deprived of anything like an adequate organ, he turned to the stringed keyboard instruments. In part this was natural: he cannot have given up improvising and practising the keyboard after all these years. Also there was the need for it: or rather needs, for his clavier music was surely written for at least two purposes. The first was as 'recital' music, though we must remember that even with a large harpsichord, sustained listening was possible only in smallish halls. Then there was educational music. His growing sons must be taught the right ways, both of playing (and Bach had unusual and forward-looking views on fingering) and composition (for he believed that for the musician the two could not be divorced). Probably he also taught some members of the nobility. To these can perhaps be added music to be played by his prince, whose interests included playing the clavier as well as the viol da gamba and other instruments.

The pressure to follow in French paths was stronger in clavier music than in any other kind, for it was only the French who had published a substantial amount of it: the Italians had concentrated on violin music, the Germans (at least those in Protestant surroundings) the organ. From d'Anglebert to François Couperin-le-Grand (whose first set of *ordres* had appeared in 1713 and whose influential *L'Art de toucher le Clavecin* was published four years later, when Bach had just arrived in Cöthen) the French had cultivated clavecin music and indeed had acquired a distinctive school of harpsichord makers, of whom the greatest was Taskin. Their favourite instrument and the music played on it had a delicacy very different from that of Italy. It was an ornamental music with an intimacy which was far from the grand public music making of Bach's organ works. Indeed, much clavecin music had acquired traits of style from the even more intimate lute, on which the necessity to break up the notes of chords rather than to play them exactly together had given rise to the so-called *style brisée*.

Bach knew such French clavecin pieces at first hand. Indeed, when compiling a book of pieces for Wilhelm Friedmann to practise, he included the list of ornaments taken from d'Anglebert. And he used these himself, notating many pieces of this era particularly with French *agréements*. The idea of writing a simple dance tune and then a 'double' or decorated version also appealed to him. He liked the *style brisée* (the famous first prelude in the first book of 'forty-eight' preludes and fugues shows its influence in the necessity to hold on to various notes instead of simply spreading the chords *ad libitum*). Yet even his most obviously French-style dances do not sound particularly French, any more than the orchestral

25

suites do. There is no piece which could possibly be taken for one by Couperin, no hint of the artifice of the Petit Trianon society. There is always a breadth of phrase, a boldness of harmony that denies the Gallic trends. There is also usually counterpoint, however discreet. It is rare for the left hand part of even a simple dance not to have its own shape, taking it from the realms of acting as bass to a tune into that of melodic pattern.

For this reason, it would be pleasant to think that the *Chromatic fantasy and fugue* belongs to those Cöthen years, even though the earliest version we possess dates from 1730 and the composition itself may well be the work of the Leipzig *Kantor*. For it reminds us of the organist, improvising an expansive preludium, then capping it with a mighty, fully worked out fugue. It is a public piece, and its cascading chromatic chords and sturdy fugue subject are not in the least speculative (as we must adjudge the concept of *The well-tempered clavier*). It is deliberately virtuosic and there is little more brilliant even in the Weimar organ music than the ultimate page, with its anchoring, satisfying pedal notes.

Most of Bach's keyboard music of this period is clearly domestic, taking the form of suites or individual dance movements, preludes and exercises in playing contrapuntal music. In his last year at Weimar, Bach had written a set of six *English suites* (there are various explanations of the title but none of them is at all satisfactory). These are successions of dances preceded by a prelude which can even be a large scale Italian concerto movement (the ones in A minor and G minor should clearly be registered on the harpsichord so as to bring out the contrasts between the imagined tutti and solos). The *French suites* have no such grand gestures. They are simply sets of dances, and the fact that the earliest source is the commonplace book kept by (or copied for) his second wife Anna Magdalena in 1722 has tempted commentators to see them as tender,

teaching pieces by an older husband and composer for a young
musical wife. But there are few signs of a systematic
instructional purpose: these are simply suites for the player's
pleasure, posing quite a few technical difficulties and
demanding utter concentration. For in spite of their title, the
suites are not graceful essays in the Gallic manner. The traditional opening movements, the allemande and courante, are
usually flurries of notes which tend to obscure the basic dance
rhythms, while the final movements are gigues after the way of
Corelli, ample structures in a bouncy triple time, but typically
Bachian in the tendency to counterpoint (which often makes
them tricky to play). The French connection may be seen more
strongly in the middle movements, the slow sarabandes which
are suitable for embellishment and the 'modern' dances, the
bourrées, the loures, the gavottes which are less adaptable to
the older polyphonic treatments and retain their essential
clarity of rhythm and texture. These indeed are charming and
suggest that in time Bach might have been absorbed by the
galant manner which was to dominate the middle decades of
the century.

But it was not to be, and the other keyboard music which he
wrote at Cöthen shows how strongly the old ways were
ingrained. There are the two- and three-part inventions he
wrote for Wilhelm Friedmann's education. Their purpose is to
make the performer capable of playing two or three independent and largely continuous strands of melody. These will
probably not have identical rhythms played simultaneously
and will almost certainly involve intricate separate fingering
patterns. In playing three independent parts, one will usually
be shared between the two hands. It is a hard discipline to learn,
especially since Bach insists on smooth legato performance of
each strand. These inventions are also lessons for the young
composer on how to write true polyphony, which is by no
means limited to fugal methods of imitative melody (though

27

imitation does occur) but in the construction of continuous melodies which are independent yet subtly dependent on each other, motifs passing from one to the other, yet without apparently deliberate intention. These melodies are frequently decorative in pattern, but the embellishments are firmly woven into the strands, so that they are essential. No wonder that these inventions are not easy to play or to imitate even today.

The other keyboard movement of this period is, strangely enough, more obviously traditional. Its title page tells us a great deal.

The Welltuned Clavier
or
Preludes, and
Fugues on all the Tones and Semitones
In both major keys or Ut Re Mi
As also in minor keys or Re Mi Fa
For the needs and use of
Musical youth, as well as those already
experienced in this study
for the passing of time, arranged
and finished by
Johann Sebastian Bach

There was, of course, no necessity to cast a series of preludes and fugues into such a format. Does one really have to be able to write in all the permutations of keys possible within the octave? Indeed, with the system of tuning which it involved whereby the octave was simply divided into twelve equal intervals, it could be held that there was no reason at all for using different keys, certainly those so near to each other for no great differences of sonority to be felt. Under the older methods of tuning, each tone and semitone was subtly different; under the new all became equal. Bach was following a not very strong tradition of publications in which composers had written in all the keys. Pachelbel (whose organ music Bach certainly admired) had written a set of suites in all the chromatic keys in 1683; and more immediately, J. C. F. Fischer had published in 1702 a collection of twenty preludes and fugues under the title *Ariadne musica*. That Bach knew this latter work is evident from the similarities of certain pieces in his 'Twenty-four' to those of Fischer. Bach, typically, is more complete (twenty-four being twelve major and twelve minor keys), even though he achieved it by transposing pieces written originally in ordinary keys into such way-out tonalities as the six sharps of the D sharp major and the six flats of the E flat minor. The result is neat (and one of the first signs of Bach's increasing concern for musical tidiness) and of course a splendid way of promoting a method of tuning which opened up new areas of modulation. For the merit of the system was not that it allowed pieces to be written in new keys. As with a powerful car, the top speed is rarely used and mainly irrelevant; but the speed of overtaking is valuable. So it is the ability to use the odd distant note, to move temporarily into a key with many sharps and flats that is the main advantage of the 'well [or rather equal] -tempered clavier'.

In fact, European music would have been very different had it not been for equal temperament: no *Tristan and Isolde*, no Schoenberg at the very least. So the 'programme' of *The well-tempered clavier* has justified itself. The actual contents need no justification of any kind. They are simply a superb collection of preludes and fugues. No doubt without his experience as an organist Bach would not have written them at all, but they are not like his earlier keyboard music in many ways. The preludes certainly belong to that tradition of improvised introductory pieces which was the stuff of a Lutheran organist's skill. Yet these are very controlled, orderly pieces. Bach will often use a harmonic pattern as a basis: then he will invent a motif to embellish it; then he will develop this motif quite intensively. The result is anything but casual – and still it seems a prelude to something else, it has no distinctive shape of its own. The technique is not very different from that of the Chopin *Etudes*, except that the motif there will be invented to emphasise the player's technical problem and will therefore have elements of bravura in it. Here there is rarely bravura, though the player may have problems enough. But the combination of improvisation and concentration is similar. The fugues, on the contrary, seem relatively relaxed. They are in no sense 'scholarly'. They use devices such as stretto, augmentation and diminution, it is true, but these concepts never dominate a piece. The fugue subjects are rarely invented to allow the display of such contrapuntal skills. Nor, like many of the Weimar organ fugue subjects, are they built around figuration to suit the fingers (curse it). Instead, they are just musically interesting, often based on a strong rhythm (dance music has after all its uses) – gigue-like metres form the basis of a couple and even a passepied in another. The result of these features is the finest polyphonic music for the player to explore by himself. They are not recital music, nor, as countless teachers of fugue have found, are they very good for instructing the pupil in fugal technique. But they remain fascinating for the player, testing his ability to play several strands in a shapely way, searching out his weaknesses in legato, yet always masterly in construction, coming to great climaxes, never overdeveloping material so that it becomes dull. No wonder that the young Beethoven found them instructive; on piano, harpsichord or clavichord they stimulate the player to utter concentration.

If this quantity of keyboard music is not surprising for one of the finest organists of his age, the paucity of true chamber music from these years reveals his isolation from that age's general trends. There are single sets of sonatas for violin and for flute with the accompaniment of a continuo team (perhaps harpsichord and cello or viola da gamba) – this at a time when the Italianate violin sonata was sweeping Europe and the so-called 'German' flute (in reality a favourite of the French, whose name 'traversière' is more apt) was becoming very popular, its one-keyed mechanism giving it an efficiency and ease of playing which made it the plaything of the amateur – especially when Frederick the Great took it up. But a look at these sonatas reveals why Bach never became very popular in these spheres. His conception was essentially that of the trio sonata, not in the sense that it needs three players, rather that there are three distinctive melodic strands: violin or flute, the right hand of the harpsichord, and the bass – this latter played either simply by the left hand of the keyboardist or with the addition of a cellist or gamba player. Contrapuntal textures are never far away, and quasi-fugal finales are in order. The problems of balance between the equal strands by the right hand on the keyboard and the other 'melody instrument' are such that even today, when 'authentic' instruments are well understood, these pieces rarely sound effective, which indicates that they must not be regarded as concert pieces, but as true chamber music. In this role they are very satisfying, being never too difficult technically nor lacking in ensemble interest – though the fact that they were more difficult and demanding than the common run of French flute music, and less virtuosic than the violin sonatas of Veracini and the rest, may account for their neglect in the eighteenth century.

More remarkable than these – perhaps more remarkable indeed than anything else written at Cöthen – are two sets of suites-cum-sonatas for unaccompanied stringed instruments, one for violin, the other for cello. There was a tradition of unaccompanied music for violin in southern Germany and Austria in the late seventeenth century, with Biber as its most famous composer; yet it cannot be said that Bach obtained anything more than the general idea from this. Similarly there was a repertoire of music for viola da gamba which might have provided some incentive to adapt its virtuoso technique to the cello (for which there are no direct antecedents). Again it is little more than the concept which has filtered through. Bach's music in this sphere is *sui generis*. There is no intrinsic reason why interesting music should not be written for single stringed instruments (much of the world's music has been either monophonic or directly related to it in the form of heterophony). What is remarkable is that such music should be written in an age in which harmony was so strongly established (for that is what the basso continuo really implies) by a man whose interests centred round polyphony. And Bach does not yield, for he writes both a chaconne and (incredibly) a fugue. The style was thus so different from anything known that when these works were revived at the end of the nineteenth century, players found them full of difficulties: and one has only to read the criticisms of G. B. Shaw to realize that even such a serious player as Joachim must have produced some appalling sounds, especially in the multiple stops, in such a piece as the fugue. So was invented the idea that they must have been written for something very unlike the modern violin, with a bow so slack that it could play on several strings at once and a rounded bridge rather than the present almost straight one. Indeed, bridges and bows were different, though not to the extent then believed; but we must suspect that the real problems came in the style of playing, for violinists and cellists are not used to playing polyphonic music as keyboard players are. For them, double or triple stops are for reinforcing chords.

Looking at the music itself, it is not these which are its main features. First comes the creation of a continuous single melodic line, which often is constructed from motifs which suggest or outline chords, so that the music sounds harmonic (Bach could thus transfer the prelude of the E major partita to orchestra and organ without a great deal of difference – and that difference is mainly sonority rather than feeling for harmony). Secondly, to give the impression of several melodic strands, he moves from different, sometimes remarkably widely apart, registers within the phrase. Between these two techniques, it is amazing how little seems to be missing: there is certainly no impression of a thin sound. When a Busoni rewrites the *Chaconne in D minor* for the grandest of pianofortes, he adds inessentials, frills and superfluous changes of sound. Bach's original contains all that is necessary by hints and suggestions. Was this public music? The suggestion has been made that Bach wrote the violin music for the virtuoso Pisendel of Dresden and this may well be so. It certainly stands up to concert performance, though the intensity for both player and listener is remarkable. The lack of distraction from other instruments or melodies gives no rest, allows for no lapses of concentration. To remark on the emotional qualities of this music is hardly possible: it is indeed music for mind as much as body.

The way this music (accompanied and unaccompanied) is grouped into sets of six, the comprehensive scheme of *The well-tempered clavier,* suggests that Bach was hoping for publication. Publishers liked volumes of six or a dozen sonatas to present to the public. J. C. F. Fischer's *Ariadne musica* had been published twenty years earlier; no doubt such publications were subsidised by the composer's patrons. Why then did not Bach receive a similar treatment? His patron was generous, and the fact that he was near no major centre of music publishing does not seem very different from Fischer's situation. Was it therefore the nature of Bach's style? Was it laziness in approaching publishers? This we shall never know.

Yet Bach seemed to be happy at Cöthen, at least during his early years there. In a letter written in 1730, he said that he 'had a gracious Prince who both loved and knew music, and in his service I intended to spend the rest of my life'. That he decided to move on may be ascribed to two facts. The first was the death of his wife. Bach went off with his master as the head of a small group of musicians to the spa at Carlsbad. When he got back to Cöthen in July 1720, she had just died and been buried. Although we have no letters or documents about their relationship, and although Bach could be a difficult man, the modern biographer has little doubt that it was a marriage of affection, at the least. Man and wife were much the same age and had had seven children. We shall see his closely knit second marriage, with its commonplace books and instruction pieces for the children, the family helping by copying parts in an emergency. There is no reason to doubt that the first marriage was dissimilar. In any case, the sudden death of a partner of like age sets one thinking of mortality and eternal life.

Bach's first reaction was to apply for a job. The organist of the Jacobikirche in Hamburg died in September. Bach was seemingly very interested in it and said so, being at this time in Hamburg. He had to go back urgently to Cöthen, but the appointing committee were still interested in him. In the end, the appointment was rigged: a nonentity was given the job – for a consideration of 4000 marks given to church funds (the writer on music, Johann Mattheson was furious and wrote a devastating column in *Der musikalische Patriot* ending with the words 'if one of the angels of Bethlehem should come down from heaven, one who played divinely and wished to become organist of St Jacobi, but had no money, he might just as well fly away again').

So he settled down again at Cöthen, with his four surviving children. Among his *Kapelle* was a young singer, Anna Magdalena Wülken, daughter of one of the trumpeters. On 3 December 1721, they were married. She kept her stipend – not an ungenerous one – at least for the next two years. The Bachs were quite well off. What finally made him discontented was that his Prince took on a wife and 'the impression should arise that the musical interests of the said Prince had become somewhat lukewarm, especially as the new Princess seemed to be unmusical', to quote Bach's own words. What was Bach to do? His hopes for promotion must by this time have diminished. Only one of the grand courts could represent a step upwards: and if nearby Dresden was an example, they would probably favour a modern opera composer. He was now in his late thirties and could not change his spots. Any other post was really a step backwards.

Then Kuhnau, *Kantor* at the Thomasschule in Leipzig died on 5 June 1722. The Town Council heard that Telemann was interested: he came, was successful; then he turned it down (his present employers at Hamburg raised his salary). They were then interested in several others including perhaps the most famous German cantata composer of the age, Graupner of Darmstadt, but he was refused permission to leave (Bach knew all about that). So, rather reluctantly, on 30 May 1723, they appointed Bach.

3 Leipzig

It pleased God that I should be called hither to be *Director Musices* and *Kantor* at the Thomasschule. Though at first, indeed, it did not seem at all proper to me to change my position of *Kapellmeister* for that of *Kantor*.

Thus Bach reflected seven years later on his decision. Although commentators since have been anxious to portray the devout German Protestant coming home to mother church after a period in unsatisfactory secular service, that is how Bach saw the change: it was a demotion. In 1730 he was still not sure why he had made the change. No doubt the call from God had had something to do with it. Certainly if the biographer wishes to find the devout German Protestant, it is only in the half dozen years from 1723 that the colours are bright. Before then, he seems a rather worldly organist and composer: from 1730 we shall see another kind of man. But in the first years at Leipzig, the religious *daemon* was in him.

The reason why by 1730 he was more than a little disillusioned was that the job was impossible – at least to do well. It was one of those posts (not rare in public service) to which duties and responsibilities had accrued over the years without anyone considering whether it was prudent for a single man to be expected to fulfil them all. It was supposed primarily to be a teaching job. Bach's predecessor had indeed been a man who has been described as one who 'displayed an element of medieval universality and mastered music, law, theology, rhetoric, mathematics and foreign languages' (Schering). Thus a little teaching of junior Latin, which is what the Council wanted of Telemann and which proved one of the sticking points leading to his refusal, should not bother the candidate. And we may suspect that a real schoolmaster was what the Council would really have liked, for when they came to replace Bach after a quarter of a century, one of the Council, the member for the War Office (presumably defence), Burgomaster Stieglitz, said that 'The School needed a *Kantor* and not a *Kapellmeister*, although he must understand music'. Indeed he had to 'understand music'! In addition to his teaching duties, the *Kantor* had to run the music at two city churches, St Thomas's and St Nicholas's, and supervise that at the New Church and St Peter's (the distinction being that he actually directed the music on alternate Sundays at the first two, whereas he merely had to see that all was well at the latter). To provide the choirs for these churches, the Thomasschule had about sixty boarders, aged from eleven to seventeen (Bach took the upper limit to twenty-one later on). The nearest equivalent to such a job today is probably the director of music at one of the colleges with a choral foundation. And while he would have a lesser number of undergraduates to teach (the boys being instructed by others in the attached school) he has to direct the music for Evensong almost every day in the chapel. Bach had only to conduct the Sunday music and that for the larger festivals of the church year – Christmas, Easter – and for civic celebrations such as the installation of a new Town Council.

But then the main Sunday service of *Hauptgottesdienst* was somewhat more demanding than that of the normal Anglican Evensong. It began at 7 a.m., the sermon lasting from eight until nine o'clock and can hardly have ended before 10.30 a.m. The order of service looks formidable (the musical items are asterisked):

*1. Organ voluntary or hymn
*2. Latin motet or organ voluntary
*3. Missa (Kyrie and Gloria)

4. 'The Lord be with you', etc.
5. Latin collect
*6. Epistle (intoned), followed by an organ interlude
7. Litany (omitted at certain festivals)
*8. Hymn (appropriate to the season)
9. Gospel (intoned)
10. Credo (intoned in Latin; omitted when there was a cantata)
*11. Cantata (described as *Stück* or *Concerto*; omitted in most of Advent and Lent)
*12. The hymn 'Wir glauben all' (Luther's metrical version of the Creed)
*13. Hymn before the sermon (followed by the gospel read in German)
14. Sermon
15. Banns of marriage.
16. Prayers
17. Intercessions and notices
*18. Hymn (related to the gospel)
19. The Lord's Prayer (intoned)
*20. Prayer of consecration and Communion (during which hymns or a Latin motet might be sung)
21. Collects (intoned)
22. Blessing (intoned)

Like his Anglican counterpart, Bach could use older music for some of these items. The motet was often chosen from the collections of Bodenschatz, one of the most diligent collectors of Italian music at the beginning of the seventeenth century, and even though the eighteenth century saw the beginnings of our modern historical approach to music, it is surprising to find music more than a century old in common use at St Thomas's. For the Mass (Kyrie and Gloria) no doubt there was an existing repertoire. But there was as yet no great printed repertoire for the cantata, especially for the grander occasions when a new work was expected. The cantata introduced other problems, including the provision of an orchestra.

Some of this could be provided by the boys: part of Bach's agreement with the Council was that he 'faithfully instruct the boys not only in vocal but also in instrumental music, so that the Churches may not have to be put to unnecessary expense'. He would also use the town-musicians, as ever, especially efficient on wind and brass; and he might find university students capable of taking part. Thus a small orchestra – but not a fully professional one – was to hand.

Seeing that all was well with the music in the churches was thus a formidable task, and no doubt Bach could have done without the teaching duties. Nevertheless, his predecessor Kuhnau had managed, apparently to the satisfaction of everyone. How? We do not know exactly how he organised his work, but it seems likely that like a good university *Informator choristarum*, he chose music which was reasonably within the capacity of his forces, bearing in mind the shortness of rehearsal time and energy. He certainly did not compose a vast quantity of new music for it – the hundred or so of his cantatas either extant or known about, hardly represent a huge quantity for a man whose career at St Thomas's had lasted over twenty years. Noticeably there is a good number of occasional pieces among them, works for the burial of the University Rector, for jubilees of churches and university, for the election of a Town Council. Thus he was by no means lazy, but concentrated on the necessities of his job; added to which he probably built up the repertoire of the choir gradually.

Not so Bach! From the start he threw all his energies into the job in a way that no man could have kept up for long. He made his first task the composition of a complete set of cantatas for every Sunday and other major festivals, a matter of about sixty for the year. He was to keep this up for five years, and although we have lost about one third of the total, we can see what this involved from the remaining two hundred, a corpus among the greater glories of European music. The idea of complete cycles of cantatas was in fashion at the time. The poet Neumeister had published the librettos for such cycles in 1711 and 1714. Telemann set to music no less than thirty-one in his years as *Kantor* at the Johanneum in Hamburg. But both Neumeister and Telemann had a far less elaborate idea of a cantata than had Bach. For Neumeister it was a piece out of an opera, a series of recitatives and arias. For Telemann it was often a piece for a solo singer. So the weekly task was not so great. If opera composers could turn out operas, amounting to perhaps forty recitatives and arias within a few weeks, surely the professional *Kantor* could compose four such recitatives and arias within the week. For Bach, the cantata must include choruses, arias frequently with complex obbligato parts, recitatives which were often 'accompanied' intricately by the orchestra. The arias were often difficult musically (also technically, but in such a weekly routine this must have seemed less important). So in place of Telemann's idea of a piece for a single voice accompanied by a continuo team, Bach composed works which would require ensemble rehearsal. We can imagine Bach's week thus. On Monday and Tuesday he must have hoped to have composed the choruses and the settings of the hymns, so that the parts could be copied in time for the choral rehearsals which probably took place from Thursday to Saturday. By Thursday, at the latest, any works with orchestra would have to be finished for their parts to be copied. If his soloists could sight read well, their music could be entrusted to them over Friday and Saturday. The final rehearsal was surely Saturday, the performance Sunday morning. Then there were weeks with special festivals: goodness knows how all that fitted in. And Bach still had his teaching duties (though he paid one of his colleagues in the school to take over some of his work there).

We can gain some idea of his energy and devotion during this period by looking at the music he wrote during his first three months at Leipzig, most of the cantatas from which period survive. He officially took up his job on 1 June 1723. On the previous Sunday, the first after Trinity, his *Die Elenden sollen essen* (BWV 75) had been given. The following Sunday *Die Himmel erzählen die Ehre Gottes* (BWV 76) was the cantata. Both these are 'double cantatas' in two parts, one for each side of the sermon. Each had a large opening chorus, two chorales, six recitatives and four arias. The famous Bach scholar W. G. Whittaker imagines the congregation coming out of St Thomas's and St Nicholas's groaning 'If only we had secured Graupner or Telemann, we wouldn't have to listen to such harsh, involved, inharmonious Hauptmusik! So terribly long too! Kuhnau's was always short and tuneful. But this man's! Whatever have we let ourselves in for!' Indeed, these pieces make few concessions to popularity. Yet the *Acta Lipsiensium Academica* remarks that 'The 30th instant [May], being the First Sunday after Trinity, the new Kantor and Director of the *Collegium Musicum*, Mr Johann Sebastian Bach, who has come hither from the Prince's Court at Cöthen, produced his first music here, with great success.' The cantata for the third Sunday after Trinity is lost, but *Ein ungefärbt Gemüthe* was performed on 20 June. This was an ordinary 'single' cantata with only two recitatives and arias, a chorus and a chorale. The chorus is not very extended, and no wonder, for the following Thursday was the feast of St John the Baptist for which Bach composed *Ihr Menschen, rühmet Gottes Liebe*, with only a concluding chorale for the chorus but two recitatives, an aria and a duet for soloists. The next few cantatas are missing but the second half of July and August saw him compose: *Erforsche mich, Gott, und erfahre mein Herz*; *Herr, gehe nicht ins Gericht*; *Schauet doch und sehet, ob irgend ein Schmerz sei*; *Siehe zu, dass deine Gottesfurcht nicht*

Heuchelei sei; *Lobe den Herrn, meine Seele*; *Du sollst Gott, deinen Herren, lieben*; *Es ist nichts Gesundes an meinem Leibe*. Most of these now have a similar format: a chorus (usually long), two recitatives and arias and a final chorale in a simple, harmonised version. This final number probably was written in a very short time, but the rest of the cantata is rarely skimped. The opening choruses often are written in some kind of fugal style or perhaps in the manner of a huge chorale prelude, both of which came naturally to the organist. The arias, on the other hand, are rarely in any customary style. They are certainly not like the simple pieces which Italian opera composers such as Bononcini and Vinci composed to delight the audiences in Venice or London. The melodies are often more complex in phrase structure, their every embellishment written out so that their character could not be ruined by the singers (as they certainly were in opera); and frequently they have obbligato parts, especially for oboe, good players of which were seemingly available in the Leipzig town music. Nor are the recitatives parlando melody accompanied by perfunctory successions of chords, but even when they are non-'accompagnati', they often contain some strange progressions sparked off by the words. So Bach's first cantata year must have been very busy, his powers of invention at their peak. For it is amazing how little Bach seems to have drawn on his previously written music in this first year. Later he borrowed freely from his own and other men's compositions, remodelling or at times adapting completely to different words. He may have used some Weimar cantatas in 1723–4; but there was little rewriting. For a man who was composing so freely and originally, inspired does not seem too strong a term.

Not that inspired work is always interesting to the outsider: the art of creation does not always succeed in communication. There are dull pieces in these cantatas, as in other works of Bach. Yet the wonder must be that in the approximately 175 cantatas that modern scholarship ascribes to these years 1723–9, so much of the music is so very fine. Perhaps this is not surprising for the opening choruses, the techniques for which came from Bach's training and experience. The use of a hymn tune as a cantus firmus for the boys to sing while the other voices weave a web of intricate polyphony; or indeed the use of each individual line of the hymn as the malleable material for successive stages of the movement combines well-tried material and well-tried formal patterns. But the beauty of the recitatives and arias came less naturally. The art of the Italianate aria of the 1730s was that of a relatively simple melody constructed in clearly defined phrases. In the da capo, the singer was encouraged to embellish, so that the sense of difficulty and climax came near the end. Bach approached the aria quite differently. He could write within such conventions: some of the arias for bass in D major sound like Handel's arias for villains or grand heroes (basses can be either) – simple in melody, because the tonality is clear. The grand *scena* for bass in the second part of *Wachet! betet! betet! wachet!* shows Bach at his most approachable. It begins with a recitative, inspired by the fate of the sinner, in which there are repeated semi-quaver chords in the strings and trumpet, with the singer using bold melodic leaps to suggest the solemnity of the situation. As the Lord hurries to judgement, so the bass breaks into semiquavers; then the mood changes to embrace the joys of the righteous, starting with a cadence on the orchestra who gradually turn to the bliss of the major key. As the singer reaches the word 'Freude' (joy) so he embarks on a huge melismatic phrase, difficult both because of the rapid speed of the notes and the large leaps. This cannot really be classified as recitative at all; it is pure textual expression, yet without the firm musical organisation of the aria. There follows a simple little ornamental aria of faith and calmness; and if it is scarcely so tuneful that it qualifies for those anthologies of arias which were copied for use in the drawing room, it is memorable enough for any congregation to appreciate. But then the reminiscences of the Last Trump are revived in the middle section; and although the consolatory mood and simplicity of tune return, the whole piece ends with a short indecisive recitative, before the final chorale.

Such are the commonplaces of Bach's cantatas of these first fruitful years at Leipzig. In retrospect they seem a marvellous collection of music in a style utterly of its own. Although Neumeister's idea of a cantata was 'a piece from an opera' and although Bach uses operatic forms they do not sound in the least operatic. And although commentators have found deep theological (and usually Protestant) meanings in Bach's music, the fact that he was capable in later years of setting new words to pre-existent music should warn us against too close an interpretation on these lines. Looking at the texts he chose to set, we can see firstly that the theological content is relatively restricted, secondly that Bach deals time after time with simple yet lively issues. Sin, death and judgement are one related group; another are the joys of Christ's birth and our redemption. Bach's Baroque poetasters or ancient hymn writers do not add very much to our conception of the Christian beliefs. Neither does Bach's music; what it frequently does is express it vividly. During *Wachet! betet! betet! wachet!*, the perils of sinning are brought in a frightening manner before the members of Bach's congregation; and also the joys of Heaven's rewards are given emotional expression in a comforting way. Indeed, comfort is the usual feeling at the end of a cantata, for the steadfast simple hymn tune is the musical equivalent of simple, steadfast Christianity.

This is how it may appear to us: how it appeared to Bach's weekly audience, the burghers of Liepzig, we may wonder. They surely enjoyed the pictorial recitatives; also the grandeur of the opening choruses; but how much they enjoyed the complex arias is another matter. They may have admired the singers – although the performances can hardly have done justice to the music. Yet they did not have our benefit of repeated hearings. After being played on one Sunday only, the music disappeared for ever, unless Bach repeated a cantata several years later, or re-used the music with a new text. Why, they may well have asked, does the man not write more obviously appealing music. The reply must be in Bach's own insignia in most of his scores: at the beginning 'J. J.' ('Jesu, Juva' – 'Jesus, help me'), at the ending 'DSGL' ('Deo soli Gloria' – 'To God alone be the glory'). For him, there was no alternative way of expressing his deeply held beliefs.

But the congregation had their rewards. If we tend to think of Bach's music as essentially concerned with the perils of Hell, it is true that certainly in his earlier years at Leipzig, Christmas acted as the inspiration of some of his finest music. His first Christmas, 1723, for example, was the occasion of his first setting of the Magnificat. He set it in sections, as the text suggests, which meant that he could use the cantata method, with a grand opening chorus followed by a succession of arias, concluding with a choral doxology. Indeed, if performed as originally (it was then in E flat only later being transposed as we normally know it today) with four chorales interposed, it becomes even nearer the Lutheran cantata. The chorus at the beginning, having no chorale as its basis, is more modern in style, seemingly owing its crisp rhythms and flowing semiquavers, its ritornello structure, to the Vivaldian concerto. The arias which follow are also simpler than usual in the cantatas, less complicated by extended ornaments and therefore more obviously attractive. The chorus to express the seeding of mankind (omnes generationes) is equally strong in rhythm and one is tempted to say that setting Latin has liberated Bach from some of his own fundamental obscurities. And indeed this view could be confirmed by another work written for the following Christmas, the *Sanctus in D major* which we now know as part of the *B minor Mass*. We do not know how this came to be written, nor why Bach apparently sent the parts to a Bohemian nobleman known to like music, the Count von Spork. It was in its original form without the section 'Pleni sunt caeli' and must have come like a bombshell in the context of even a festive service, after the preacher had read his lengthy *praefationes* for the communion. It is especially astonishing because it lasts so little time, precluding any real manipulation of material or use of the devices which Bach, the polyphonist, favoured. Indeed, when later he completed the *B minor Mass* he was careful to set the 'Pleni sunt caeli' as an extended polyphonic section. The 'Sanctus' itself is just a blaze of glory, high trumpets, oboes, six-part choir all placed so as to make the most of their most brilliant registers. The rhythms are those of gigues, and indeed this is one of the greatest Dances of God. But this has tempted modern interpreters, trying to get away from the solemnities of romantic 'religious' interpretations, to take it at a gigue-like speed. The weight of sound really precludes this: in a lively church acoustic, too fast a tempo means a jumble, where this piece must be clear and bell-like. This 'Sanctus' is a few minutes of pure revelation. It cannot be explained or analysed, and it is a pity that today it is heard in concert performances of a piece that was never so designed: for at the least, the choir will be tired, and at the most, the surrounding music does not allow for this suddenness of revelation.

If this is the most sublime piece of Bach's first year at Leipzig, the greatest sustained work is undoubtedly his setting of the *Passion according to St John*, formerly believed to have been performed as a kind of *vorspeise*, composed at Cöthen for Easter 1723, some months before he took up his job at Leipzig, nowadays believed to have been written for Easter 1724. If this is true, it was given in St Nicholas's rather than St Thomas's in spite of Bach's preference for the latter, but he agreed provided that the harpsichord should be repaired and that 'a little additional room be provided in the choir loft, so he could place the persons needed for the music'. This latter request seems to denote that the performance was a greater enterprise than usual: and so it must surely have been. For although many people think of this as Bach's 'little' passion, that is only because the *St Matthew Passion* of five years later is a colossus. Not that quite large-scale Passion Music of various kinds was abnormal in Lutheran churches of the time. The idea of dramatising the events of Holy Week of course goes back to the Middle Ages, if not earlier, the parts of the various protagonists being sung by different singers in plainchant. But it was only with the birth of opera and its attendant oratorio that the chances for a really vivid dramatisation in music became apparent. There were by Bach's time two main ways of treating the story. The first was simply to turn it into an oratorio, getting a poetaster to provide a libretto with recitatives and arias just as in an opera, except that there will be a narrator to tell the story. This was the Hamburg way, as might be expected in a city where there was vernacular opera. There Keiser and Handel set the Brockes libretto. A criticism of this by severe Protestants might be that levelled at Elgar's works a couple of centuries later: that it 'stank of incense'. And indeed this must have sounded very like Roman Catholic music, and its concentration on humankind rather than the divine story might well have disturbed those who wished to exclude anything secular. At Leipzig, such full scale Latinisms were out of order and they preferred what one might call the oratorio-ised Passion. This took the biblical words as a basis for the story telling, adding arias (to a written text by the kind of poet who wrote cantatas) commenting on it, and inserting hymns. The crowd, fickle between the cheering of Christ and its preference for

Barabbas was naturally taken by the chorus. Kuhnau provided an example of this kind in 1721, which included no less than twenty hymns and eighteen arias, the latter quite simple and certainly not in the operatic style of Hamburg. One wonders whether this had provoked the comment of one of the Town Councillors on Bach's appointment that he hoped the new *Kantor* would not provide 'theatrical music'. Nevertheless there must have been a faction that encouraged Bach to write something similar, otherwise he would hardly have embarked on such a huge piece at a time when he was already busy with cantatas. He knew some modern Passion music already, including Handel's piece setting Brockes. He indeed added eight textual insertions of Brockes to the text of the Bible. There was now no question of him going too far for the Leipzig burghers, for he can have known little truly operatic music. In the end, he went the way we might expect from an experienced cantata composer, using chorales, arias and choruses very elaborately.

There is, of course, one difference. Cantatas do not tell a story: the Passion is a story. And it is an extraordinarily gripping one. Compared with this, the libretti of contemporary operas seem feeble and slow moving. By choosing the Gospel of St John, Bach was choosing the most concise version, starting with the arrest of Jesus to his death on the cross and subsequent burial. The scenes of Peter's denial, Jesus' trial and the crucifixion itself are all highly dramatic, and if St Matthew's Gospel offers more detail and preparation, that of St John offers more opportunities to show both the crowd's cruelty and Pilate's decency. It is not, perhaps, the obvious version to set to music simply because it truncates comment.

Bach should not surprise us by the quality of his music: the surprise comes in his understanding of dramatic pace. Certainly there is no lack of contemplative music, both in choruses and arias; but it is noticeable in the latter that Bach avoids the da capo, or repeat, convention, so that they are not expanded to the usual proportions. They are still in the cantata style with complex vocal lines and sometimes there are fine obbligato parts, using viole d'amore, viole da gamba and even a lute. The opening and closing choruses, the opening and closing of the curtains on the play as it were, caused Bach some trouble before he finally settled on two large-scale pieces which now seem utterly natural, first to set the scene, finally to provide a comment to set the events within the wider framework of church ritual. Yet in the end, it is not the consoling element which the listener remembers but the inhumanity of the crowd, the cruelty of man. The chorales, presumably for the congregation to sing, are very beautifully and aptly harmonised and seem chosen to underline the fact that this is our cruelty, our responsibility. Performed without the religious solemnity of Victorian and Edwardian times, given not necessarily fast, rather with a sense of the drama, the narration leaves us in a state of shock. Bach does it without exaggerated word painting (though the jagged accompaniment of the scourging scene is indeed anguishing), knowing that the words themselves, heightened by appropriate musical pitch, will do their work. The total is indeed baroque, in the sense of juxtaposing elements to disturb, to heighten emotion. The realism of the vision at first may seem rather like the wooden crucifixes in Southern German and Austrian churches with the crown of thorns, the worn, tired face of Jesus carved in almost shocking detail. But Bach's *Passion* is still more vivid, for it depicts the building-up to that state. Maybe such a Passion play as that at Oberammergau, given before the days of great publicity and worldly grandeur, might be a better comparison; even then, Bach's vision is more sophisticated, more suited to drive home the lesson.

Concert performances of Bach's *Passions* distort our view of his Christianity, because the works are abstracted from their liturgical context. On Easter Sunday there is the cantata again, and probably on the Monday too, when in 1724 it may well have been *Erfreut euch, ihr Herzen* (BWV 66), adapted, so it seems (and who is to blame Bach), from a serenata originally written for the birthday of the Cöthen prince in 1718. Surely this is a deliberately uplifting piece, with its trumpet and the setting of that most splendid of Easter hymns, *Christ ist erstanden*.

There are no personal letters and few documents to tell us much about Bach's life at this time, but it is easy to imagine that it was a happy period for him. The amount of work he completed must have kept him almost totally occupied. During the first two years at Leipzig almost certainly he wrote a cantata each week. In the third year (1725–6) it seems to have eased off a little, and he used more of other men's music. From 1727, although much of the music he wrote is lost, he received a new incentive towards cantata composition from meeting a local teacher and poet, Christian Friedrich Henrici (*nom de plume* Picander) who in 1728 published a set of *Cantaten auf die Sonn-und Fest-Tage*, in the preface of which he wrote that 'the lack of poetic charm may be compensated by the beauty of the music of our incomparable *Kapellmeister* Bach', an assessment which seems just enough from those poems and compositions which survive. Apart from work for St Thomas's, Bach had a growing family to enjoy. Anna Magdalena's second commonplace book was started in 1725 and shows his concern for it. There are more suites for keyboard, a cantata, an 'aria' which was later to be adorned with many variations (we know it in its 1741 version as the theme of the *Goldberg Variations*), some pieces by the older sons, a beautiful aria 'Bist du bei mir' – now believed to be not by Bach but his contemporary Stöltzel – and sundry chorale settings. This was surely the repertoire for the next generation of the dynasty, serious as ever, craftsmanlike as ever, and, it must be said, as unfashionable as ever. This fact is underlined by Bach's first essays as a publisher, for in 1726 he began printing, one by one, a set of partitas. A more famous man, certainly a more fashionable one would not have had to undertake this himself: the great publishing houses of Holland or England would surely have done the work for him. It is typical that this first publication was of partitas, a genre which is a kind of suite. The difference between suite and partita in the early eighteenth century was that the former had the suggestion of the dances of the French overture, *galant* and ornamental, while the latter was of Germanic origin, based on the seventeenth-century idea of variation, whereby having written, say, an allemande, the courante would use the same tune and harmonies but put to them a different rhythm. In fact, Bach's partitas are not particularly German, although he uses suggestions of thematic alterations. But he is not averse to using a French overture (the second partita opens with a massive one) while there are sparkling examples of modern techniques (the gigue of the first partita uses constant crossing of hands in the way common in the sonatas of Domenico Scarlatti). Yet on the whole, there is little resemblance to popular *galanterie*. These are serious instrumental pieces, suitable for family or the pupils in St Thomas's.

The climax of the music of Bach's middle years must be accounted the *Passion according to St Matthew*, which seems to have been given first on Good Friday, 1727, or possibly 1729. By either year, the Leipzig congregation would have had time to get used to the 'theatrical' style. The *St John Passion* had been repeated with various alterations in 1725; while Picander seems to have written another Passion text around that time which may have been set by Bach. The *St Matthew Passion* is a much more consciously organised affair than the St John had been. Picander wrote all the non-biblical interpolations; and whereas Bach had been careful to use relatively small resources in 1724, by the writing of the *St Matthew* he had been emboldened so much that he composed for double choir and orchestra. The idea no doubt came from the traditional motet which had often been a double choir work, to which genre Bach had already added a double choir example, *Fürchte dich nicht*, possibly written for a memorial service in 1726. And in May 1727 he was to provide the mightiest of all his motets *Singet dem Herrn ein neues Lied*, possibly for the birthday of Friedrich August, King of Poland and Elector of Saxony. But the *St Matthew Passion* was written more elaborately than even these, for its double choir and orchestra need not only twice twenty singers but two orchestras of at least a dozen each, of distinctive constitution. How these forces were divided spatially is not known. A century earlier there would certainly have been some attempt at making a substantial gap between them: but they may have all been crowded into the relatively small space of the organ gallery at St Thomas's. Be that as it may, the *St Matthew Passion* is written on the largest scale of all Bach's works for Leipzig churches, a fact also reflected in its very length which is substantially greater than that of the *St John Passion*.

In part this increase in length is due to the greater length of the account in St Matthew's Gospel. This begins with the events leading up to the arrest of Jesus: the plotting of the chief priests, the effect on Judas, the Last Supper and the Agony in the Garden. Certainly the trial offers less scope in this version than in St John's. But the increase in length is also due to a somewhat different attitude which results in more meditative pieces proportionally to the narrative. The Last Supper is in itself capable of stimulating a meditation: the Agony in the Garden is a meditation. Maybe because Picander was to hand and could suggest things which a composer by himself could not imagine, maybe because Bach was now less seriously 'realistic', the *St Matthew Passion* gives a greater impression of contemplation than it does of drama. Not that realism is absent. The evangelist's melismatic expression of Peter's denial and his weeping; the grand cry of 'Barabbas' from the crowd at Pilate's question; the earthquake and the release of the dead from their graves at the crucifixion do not yield in their dramatic impact. Nevertheless the grand choruses, the arias, several of which use the da capo form, and most especially and masterly use of chorales make the *St Matthew Passion* the finest meditation on the sinful nature of Man and of God's goodness. Again the congregation is involved in the action. Can the Christian deny, when one of the disciples, told by Jesus that one of them will betray him, asks 'Lord, is it I?', that the following hymn verse, 'Tis I whose sin now binds Thee', applies not just to a person long ago in a far-off land, but also to him in St Thomas's 1700 years after the event? If the *St John Passion* may remind us of the realistic wooden crucifixes of Southern Germany, the *St Matthew* seems to be the counterpart of the illustrations of great Missals or Bibles, drawing the reader's attention to the significance of the events, though again, it is more vivid than these, for Bach's story-telling makes it so.

There are tell-tale signs that by 1729 Bach was undergoing some form of change of life. Firstly, as far as we can tell, the composition of the weekly cantata ceased. Then there are documents which speak of Bach's dissatisfactions with the arrangements for the music at the churches under his control. There were all kinds of niggling arguments between *Kantor* and Council in the next years. He even seems to have started to search for a new job. In Leipzig, he took on the directorship of the University Collegium Musicum. Some part of this change can perhaps be ascribed to his natural restlessness. After all, he had rarely kept a job for more than six years (Weimar was the exception, with just nine years). But this was something bigger in Bach's life.

The explanation of the giving up of cantata composition could be simply that he was tired and now had a vast repertoire to choose from. Yet the same could have been true of Telemann who continued long after he had composed a substantial repertoire. Moreover, weekly habits die hard, and it is very difficult to believe that Bach saw it that way. It is noticeable that we possess scarcely more than a dozen church cantatas from the remaining twenty years of his life: and these (as well as other church music) tend to be reworkings (indeed total adaptations, in some cases) of previously composed music. Had the spark burned out? No doubt his complaints about conditions were connected. Here for six years he had sweated to compose sophisticated music for the Leipzig congregations. For this, the elders had provided him with totally inadequate resources. Bach wrote what he called 'a short but most necessary draft for a well-appointed church music; with certain modest reflections on the decline of the same'; but it can hardly have seemed either short or modest to the Town Councillors. It was in fact a cry of anguish. There were not enough singers and the selection of boys for the Thomasschule did not give enough attention to their musical talents. Moreover, that they are ill equipped on joining the school means that there is not enough time to instruct them properly. There are not enough instrumentalists among the town musicians, and although he had persuaded university students to take part, he cannot offer them honoraria to keep them. So it goes on. His demands of course are modest: he only wants forty-four singers (and yet can raise just seventeen competent and another twenty who will in time be competent). He only wants another eleven instrumentalists to complete his orchestra. To those nineteenth-century commentators who had just discovered Bach's greatness, the meanness of the Town Council was still more evidence that genius was insulted. In fact, the Town Council wanted a *Kantor* and received a *Kapellmeister*. Perhaps even Bach now realised his mistake: he was no *Kantor* but certainly a *Kapellmeister*. So he wrote the letter to Georg Erdmann, Imperial Russian Agent in Danzig, from which we have already quoted at the beginning of this chapter. He recalled his doubts about moving from Cöthen to Leipzig and seems now to regret his decision. So he records his disappointments:

Here by God's will, I am still in service, but since (1) I find that the post is by no means so lucrative as it had been described to me; (2) I have failed to obtain many of the fees pertaining to the office; (3) the place is very expensive; and (4) the authorities are odd and little interested in music, so that I must live amid almost continual vexation, envy, and persecution.

So he asks his old school friend from Lüneburg whether he knows of any possible post in Danzig.

It was hardly likely. Bach, in the event, had to seek consolation at home, apparently finding it to some degree in taking on the Collegium Musicum. Perhaps this lively little ensemble of university folk reminded him of his days in Cöthen (where he had recently been back to conduct the funeral music for Prince Leopold). Anyway, he began to provide a repertoire of concertos for its weekly concerts. He used some of his Cöthen material, arranging earlier music for the new circumstances, as well as composing new pieces. Among the new works were two more suites, one the grand French-style overture in D major for full orchestra, in which the dance material included the famous air, arranged quite unnecessarily by Wilhelmj for playing on the G string, in its original version simply a very beautiful decorative aria in Bach's customary style, the phrases spun out delicately to form that seamless melody which confounded singers by its lack of breathing pauses, but goes well on violins. Sometime in the late 1730s, he wrote the B minor Suite for flute and strings, more obviously in the French style (the solo instrument being a great favourite at

55

Versailles) with a decorative rather than a powerful overture, followed by some *galant*-ish dances. He also wrote some sonatas for flute and a certain amount of other chamber music.

But the real achievement of these years with the Collegium Musicum was the composition of a large number of concertos, most of which survive in arrangements for keyboard and strings, although many of them probably started life in versions for violin and oboe used either solo or together. It is fitting that they exist today in harpsichord versions, for it was Bach's unique achievement to have seen the possibility of this particular genre, and without his works, passed on to the community at large by his sons, it is quite possible that the vast repertoire of the piano concerto would not have come about. The reason why Bach should be first in this particular field may well be fortuitous. The concerto had been invented by Italian violinists; no substantial school of keyboard players existed in Italy, while the great German organists were quite content with their own instrument in churches. So Bach, the organist but also the *Kapellmeister* and the father of several good harpsichordists (both C. P. E. and W. F. were clearly developing into fine players) was the logical man to discover the potentialities.

These potentialities are largely those of scale and sonority. Scale does not mean length: after all, these harpsichord concertos were mainly arrangements from concertos which still took Vivaldi as the model. But the two hands of the keyboard player allow for counterpoint and hence closer argument of themes than lyrical oboists and violinists enjoy. Themes tend towards the complexity of Bach's organ music rather than to follow the essential simplicity of the Italian school, and decorative lines are added as counterparts to the main melodic lines, as though Bach could not resist elaboration. A good example of the expansion of ideas is to be found at the opening of the famous D minor Concerto for a single harpsichord, which although it probably began as a violin concerto (much of the virtuoso figuration suggests the cross-string writing so common after Vivaldi), seems to be the archetypal keyboard concerto. The opening ritornello theme is long and complex: it has the Vivaldian internal repetitions to aid the memory, but each segment of the theme could have come out of a keyboard fugue, and it is certainly more weighty than Italian themes commonly are. For this reason, even though it is no longer than the ordinary ritornello, it seems it. The weightiness continues with the entry of the harpsichord whose figuration is more elaborate (deriving from music in which the keyboard instrument is totally alone and must perforce be fuller); and the combined sophistication of the ritornello material and this keyboard manner result in an ampleness which makes the Italian models appear lightweight indeed.

In the concertos for several keyboards this shows even more firmly. No doubt Bach got the idea for such concertos when he transcribed Vivaldi's famous Concerto in B minor for solo violins from *L'Estro Armonico* – and it must be said that Bach's transcription (in A minor) turns a piece perfectly written for its medium into something rather lumpy and heavy. But when he puts the idea to his own use, heaviness turns into grandness, especially in the last movements which change from Vivaldi's throw away dances into climactic finales of a most exciting order. One such is the concerto for three claviers in C major, where the finale consists of a vast ritornello movement in which, within the main theme, each player in turn shows his skill. It is surely a concerto for the Bach family. The first soloistic episode was perhaps for Carl Philipp Emanuel, no mean player, who is given some intricate but not outstandingly difficult fioritura. The second (for Wilhelm Friedmann?) is distinctly more difficult and brilliant. Then comes the old man's episode, an astonishing flurry of semiquavers demanding extraordinary facility – and creating intense excitement resolved only by a straightforward final restatement of the ritornello. The surprising feature of this movement is that it does not give the impression of being virtuosic: the idea of each episode being harder technically than the previous one is a grandly designed crescendo. The nature of the figuration itself, like Mozart's a half century later, is well organised and there are no merely brilliant arpeggios (a fact which makes each part more difficult to play than it sounds). Better still is the finale of the C major concerto for two claviers, a fugue for two harpsichords (the orchestra is not strictly necessary) of close thematic argument and power which again gives a climax to an already large-scale work. If there is a weakness in these concertos it lies usually in the slow movements, where the violin's capacity for sweetly singing melody has had to be replaced by a finicky, spun out line, sometimes beautiful but lacking that lyrical quality which would have made these concertos more even in expression – and more popular.

For the sad fact is that these concertos, however well they were received at the Collegium Musicum, did nothing for Bach's wider reputation. No Amsterdam publisher or Walsh of London or indeed a local house at Dresden or Leipzig took them up. At a time when Vivaldi's concerto sets were still going the rounds (and those of many more minor figures), Bach was yet unknown. Having had no response from Danzig, he was clearly still on the look-out for a new job. There is evidence of his continuing dissatisfactions at home. A copy of a Bible with the annotations of the seventeenth-century theologian Abraham Calov is dated 1733 with his monogram JSB on the title pages of the three volumes. Bach's own underlinings and comments are to be found. They have been used to show Bach's continuing faith and deep knowledge of the Bible; but coming from the hand of such a seasoned campaigner, they look all too clearly like the texts to be used in a coming battle against the unmusical members of the Town Council. This is the comment on Chapter XXV of the First Book of Chronicles, in which King David provides the 'two hundred, fourscore and eight musicians' who shall praise the Lord in the Temple: 'This chapter is the true foundation of all church music pleasing to God'. And to encourage himself in the battle, Bach has underlined a comment by Calov: 'but where your service to your profession demands it, there you must be angry'.

An even clearer indication of Bach's state of mind about Leipzig comes in a letter which he sent with a manuscript copy of a Kyrie and Gloria to the Elector of Saxony, a document so revealing and personal that it must be read in full:

To your Royal Highness I submit in deepest devotion the present slight labour of that knowledge which I have achieved in *musique*, with the most wholly submissive prayer that Your Highness will look upon it with Most Gracious Eyes, according to Your Highness's World-Famous Clemency and not according to the poor *composition*; and thus deign to take me under Your Most Mighty Protection. For some years and up to the present moment I have had the *Directorium* of the Music in the two principal churches in Leipzig, but have innocently had to suffer one injury or another, and on occasion also a diminution of the fees accruing to me in this office; but these injuries would disappear altogether if Your Royal Highness would grant me the favour of conferring upon me a title of Your Highness's Court Kapelle, and would let Your High Command for the issuing of such a document go forth to the proper place. Such a most gracious fulfilment of my most humble prayer will bind me to unending devotion, and I offer myself in most indebted obedience to show at all times, upon Your Royal Highness's Most Gracious Desire, my untiring zeal in the composition of music for the church as well as for the orchestra, and to devote my entire forces to the service of Your Highness, remaining in unceasing fidelity.

Your Royal Highness's most humble and most obedient slave

Johann Sebastian Bach

Dresden, July 27, 1733

The resentment over suffering 'one injury or another', the let down (as he probably felt it) over the fees promised when he left his *Kapellmeister*-ship to come to be a *Kantor*; above all, the desire for status ('a title of Your Highness's Court *Kapelle*') have welled up again.

The 'poor composition' which he had sent as an example of his music are what we know today as the first two movements of the *B minor Mass*. The choice was nicely made. Dresden was a Roman Catholic court to which a Mass came well – and since the *Hauptgottesdienst* at Leipzig also included the Mass (albeit only the Kyrie and Gloria of the original ceremonial, as we saw at the beginning of this chapter) Bach was used to composing in this genre. But more than that, Bach shows himself aware of the particular requirements of a modern Roman Catholic chapel by producing two movements in the latest Italian manner, the so-called 'Neapolitan Mass'. This was the kind of 'cantata' Mass favoured by the products of the Neapolitan conservatoires, the composers who were sweeping Europe with their operas. The idea was that each section of the Mass was divided into movements complete in themselves. Thus the Kyrie could be divided into three parts: (i) Kyrie I, which might be set as a chorus, (ii) Christe eleison, which might be set as a solo aria or duet, (iii) Kyrie II, which might well be a choral fugue. The longer texts, such as the Gloria and Credo, would be split into many more movements. The solos naturally took on something of an operatic flavour, for this was, after all, the common style of the time. The choruses were often contrapuntal, since the Neapolitan *maestri* insisted on their pupils learning a kind of bastardised sixteenth-century style; but they would also be *concertante*, with contrasts between soloists and tutti. The resources for performing such works were ample, with the castrati and tenors of the opera house joining in with a presumably less brilliant choir but a very competent orchestra. This was the stuff for Dresden, that most Italianate of courts where a German, Johann Adolf Hasse, was now in charge of the music. But what a German! He had spent the last few years in Italy, at Naples and Venice, had acquired an Italian wife (the renowned opera singer Faustina), was a Roman Catholic convert, and was indeed musically speaking, the most Italianised composer of northern Europe. Thus Bach must surely write a 'Neapolitan Mass'.

Neapolitan in manner; not in the least in style. Bach's Mass is so unlike the generality of Italian church music, that the Saxony Elector's musical advisers must have been considerably baffled by this intricate score (it seems not to have procured Bach's asked-for title). Surely, the resources were right: soloists, large choir and an orchestra which included trumpets. Surely the overall division into sections was right (although there are one or two unusual things here). But the attitude is wrong. This *Kantor* has been too immersed in German Protestant music to follow the more agreeable ways of Italian church music.

Truly he begins well with a grand declamation of the words 'kyrie eleison' (in fact it is an elaborate harmonisation of Luther's own intonation in his *German Mass* of 1525). But then he goes into a lengthy fugue, not on any conventional *stile antico* subject in the way of Neapolitan composers, rather on one constructed on a 'sob' motif of the kind one finds for expressing grief in the cantatas. The construction of the fugue seems vaguely like that of a concerto movement, with episodes and a recapitulation of the ritornello-fugue theme, but the scale is vast. Relief comes with the 'Christe eleison' which is a duet for soloists and more obviously attractive. Then, with the return of 'Kyrie', he embarks on another fugue, not this time on the enormous scale of the first, and indeed as it is in the *stile antico*, it seems nearer to Naples and ready appreciation. In fact, again the subject is a tortuous one (it winds round a single note in a tense, chromatic way) and the argument is close and eschews *concertante* episodes.

The 'Gloria' must have seemed more to Saxon taste, for it opens with a splendid orchestral ritornello which the choir takes up as though in an Italian concerto (and Vivaldi was well known in Dresden). Strangely Bach decides not to develop it to the full, pulling away from its liveliness to introduce the words 'Et in terra pax' where he works out a 'rest' motif over slow-moving bass notes. After this chorus, comes an aria for 'Laudamus te' and from then on a succession of solos and choruses. We recognise the style of the solo sections from the cantatas: whether the Catholic masters at Dresden would have done is more doubtful, for they are certainly not the ordinary, virtuoso arias of Italy. The melody is usually intricate and Bach's liking for obbligato instruments is exploited. Of the choruses, the old style counterpoint of 'Gratias agimus' would not have seemed too extraordinary, nor perhaps the vigorous concerto-like 'Cum Sancto Spiritu'. What, on the other hand, Bach's listeners would have made of the section setting 'Quoniam tu solus sanctus' can surely be imagined. Here a bass voice contests ('accompanied' is certainly the wrong word) two bassoons and a *corno da caccia*, together with a continuo team of, presumably, cello, bass and organ. Historically this weird sound can be explained as an example of the German liking for 'wind choirs' which dates back to the early seventeenth century at least. Yet there was nothing like it in the eighteenth century and the listeners, if there were any, at Dresden would have been completely baffled; even today, with our tolerant ears to unusual combinations, it still sounds very strange.

Was this *Missa* ever performed at Dresden? It seems

unlikely. One would like to think that these great movements were heard at least at St Thomas's as part of Bach's usual activities, perhaps at Christmas or on Easter Day. In any case, Bach was not finished with his 'High Mass' which will be discussed further, later in these pages. Nor was Bach finished with the wooing of the Elector of Saxony. He composed a dozen works in the next few years for royal celebrations of various kinds. On one occasion indeed the Elector came to Leipzig, for which Bach composed a celebratory piece only to have to cobble up another, very quickly, when the royalty actually arrived a few days early. On this occasion we have a description of the way the music was given. It was nine o'clock in the evening, the concert lit by candles held by six hundred students. The *Abendmusik* used trumpets and drums, and was heard by the royal party at the window, the performers being outside, and, says the report with apparent surprise, the royal guests listened until the end. These ceremonial pieces are usually included among Bach's cantatas, but they are better seen as serenatas. The texts, some of them by Bach's usual librettist Picander, are miniature plays, Gods and Goddesses praising indirectly the virtues of the Saxon monarch. The verse, though of no great poetic quality, has several attractions, not least that there is quite a lot of opportunity for word painting; and Bach proves, as ever, capable of turning his hand to a new genre, for his sense of open-air sonorities, especially trumpets and drums, shows him enjoying the opportunity for splendid sound. Much of the music of these serenatas turns up in other contexts, notably the *Christmas Oratorio*, so much so that some devout scholars of the past have suggested that Bach borrowed from the religious pieces, since the quality of the choruses is especially so good (the discussions centring on the 'virginity' of the *Christmas Oratorio* would make one think that the Holy Church was as attractive as devotional interpretations of the

Song of Songs made her out to be). But it is difficult to believe that the opening chorus of Part I of the *Christmas Oratorio* was not composed first for *Tönet, ihr Pauken! Erschallet, Trompeten!*, since that is precisely what happens – a strong rhythmic figure from the drums, followed by fanfares from the trumpets. And the 'Osanna' in the final version of the *B minor Mass*, finished in the next decade, seems an equally appropriate specimen of these al fresco entertainments.

Bach received his reward in 1736 when he was at last made 'Court Composer' and went to pay his respects by giving a recital on the new Silbermann organ at the Frauenkirche in Dresden. By that time, Leipzig had heard the *Christmas Oratorio*, not an oratorio in the usual eighteenth-century sense, which meant to all intents a sacred opera without costumes, but a series of six cantatas, given on various days between Christmas Day 1734 and Epiphany (January 6) 1735. Whether taken from other sources or not, the music is magnificent, a great antidote to the picture of Bach the lover of death, and the musician of the Passions. Here he loves birth (there is a rare tenderness in a number of movements) and the Saving of the World by the word incarnate. What the *Christmas Oratorio* is not, is dramatic. Though the series of scenes which it paints tell a story, there is little sense of movement, no feeling of urgency. This, and the circumstances for which it was written, make it difficult to sense it as a grand unified work – while its length precludes performance at a single sitting. Yet it is essentially a progression of cantatas, to give just two or three of which leaves a feeling of dissatisfaction. As so often with Bach's work, it fits its circumstances so perfectly that our efforts to transplant never quite succeed.

By the time he had been given his title by the Elector of Saxony, Bach needed some moral support, for he was having a terrible row with the new headmaster of the Thomasschule. The facts are fairly clear. The Head Prefect had flogged one of the junior boys so severely that the prefect had to be dismissed. This the headmaster did. Then he appointed a new Head Prefect, without consulting Bach; and since he was not particularly musical, he appointed someone who was not Bach's own favourite. But Bach needed prefects who could conduct (the only way he could keep the music going at four churches each Sunday was to have such prefects). So there was a row. Documents flew, arguments and precedents were deployed, the Town Council petitioned and eventually the affair had to be settled in Dresden. It was clearly one of those situations in which law and precedents did not help, for the *sine qua non* of smooth administration is that colleagues consult and arrive at a compromise solution. No doubt the headmaster was at fault; but Bach standing on his dignity cannot have helped and his reputation as a difficult man was probably consolidated.

And now we detect yet another change in Bach's attitude to life. He was over fifty. Two of his sons, Wilhelm Friedmann and Carl Philipp Emanuel were out in the world. It was unlikely that he was going to change his job, a job with which he was evidently disillusioned. Now came a discouragement from another quarter. A criticism of his work was published in a Hamburg journal:

Finally, Mr ––– is the most eminent of the *Musikanten* in –––. He is an extraordinary artist on the clavier and on the organ, and he has until now encountered only one person with whom he can dispute the palm of superiority. I have heard this great man play on various occasions. One is amazed at his ability and one can hardly conceive how it is possible for him to achieve such agility, with his fingers and with his feet, in the crossings, extensions, and extreme jumps that he manages, without mixing in a single wrong tone, or displacing his body by any violent movement.

This man would be the admiration of whole nations if he had more amenity (*Annehmlichkeit*), if he did not take away the natural element in his pieces by giving them a turgid (*schwülstig*) and confused style, and if he did not darken their beauty by an excess of art. Since he judges according to his own fingers, his pieces are extremely difficult to play; for he demands that singers and instrumentalists should be able to do with their throats and instruments whatever he can play on the clavier. But this is impossible. Every ornament, every little grace, and everything that one thinks of as belonging to the method of playing, he expresses completely in notes; and this not only takes away from his pieces the beauty of harmony but completely covers the melody throughout. All the voices must work with each other and be of equal difficulty, and none of them can be recognised as the principal voice. In short, he is in music what Mr von Lohenstein was in poetry. Turgidity has led them both from the natural to the artificial, and from the lofty to the sombre; and in both one admires the onerous labour and uncommon effort – which, however, are vainly employed, since they conflict with nature.

The writer was Johann Adolph Scheibe and the notice was published in Scheibe's own journal the *Critischer Musikus*. This was a recently established periodical and one might well ask whether it had any real status at all. Nevertheless, music criticism was rare at that time, and was evidently taken seriously. J. S. Bach did not reply to this article, but he can scarcely have ignored it, for several of his supporters took his part and wrote rebuttals. In fact, there was a first-class discussion, of a type better known in France than in Germany.

Scheibe's criticism can only be understood against the background of what one might call the 'aesthetic of Baroque music' – or, to narrow the context to Germany the 'theory of the affections'. The basis of this theory – or rather, theories, for there was no universally accepted attitude – goes back to the Renaissance search for the marvels of the Ancients, the greatness of a music which could stir men to War or Love, cure the sick and all the other mind-boggling tricks which could be found in Classical texts and even the Bible. Since the Greeks seemed to have found that certain modes or scales moved one or other of the passions (or 'humours', to quote the very relevant sixteenth-century medical terminology) it was agreed that a set of musical figures could fulfil this function for the modern composer. Such speculation was popular among the Italian theorists of the sixteenth century, and was the basis of some of Monteverdi's experiments, notably those of the *stile concitato* or 'agitated style' (best seen in *Il Combattimento di Tancredi e Clorinda*) in which rhythmic patterns seemingly advocated by Plato were used.

But it was the Germans who, late to take to the idea, nevertheless codified musical figuration and promulgated the methods of 'moving the affections'. The first thing to do was to decide which 'humour' was involved. That was not always an easy task with modern theological poets, said the theorist Heinichen, and one even had to search for the Biblical source of the idea to decide. Having done that, the composer must invent a suitable musical motif or idea which fits the 'humour'. In practice there were a number of such stock figures – vigorous rhythmic themes for anger or aggression, chromatic progressions for lamenting, lyrical melodies for happiness and so on. Then the composer must develop the theme. This was the hard bit, for the whole aria or movement must be imbued with the theme which must not be superseded or replenished by different material at whim. But like a good orator (and the art of oration was the one which musical theorists took as an analogy), the composer's exploration of his chosen theme would be the way to move the hearer – to Devotion in this context rather than to Love or War.

When these theories were rediscovered by the commentators on Bach in the later nineteenth century, they were grasped as the solution to the composer's mind. Surely everything, his approach to Protestant theology and indeed life in general could be deduced from his expression of the 'affection'. Today it scarcely seems so simple. For one thing, Bach sometimes uses music set to one set of words to set an entirely different text with even a different 'affect'. For another thing, such theories were really developed to help the composers of opera seria (they are much easier to apply to Handel) and certainly of less than universal application.

That Bach was aware of such theories is indisputable, how far he followed them is open to debate. The idea of the 'affect' can be most easily seen in his chorale preludes, where he takes the 'humour' of the hymn text, frequently inventing a very appropriate motif which he works out in detail, to the immense benefit of the chorale, since its inner meaning is borne to the listener in the most vivid way. Elsewhere, it is harder to see the 'affect' since the thematic material of, say, a concerto movement is not identifiable. Nevertheless, the general attitude encouraged by the 'affections' theory is very much Bach's. He loves to invent a motif which he then develops to the limit. He loves the intricacy of intellectual workmanship which is involved. And this is precisely why he fell foul of Scheibe.

Scheibe has had a poor press. He has been accused of a vengeful stab in the back (he had applied for the job of organist at the Nicolaikirche but not been awarded it by a board which included Bach) and simple blindness in the face of a great genius. But his criticism is not only understandable from the point of view of 1737: it is also quite incisive. He looks at Bach's music from the 'modern' point of view, the view of a man who sees that music is becoming *galant*. He is the follower of Hasse and the others who wrote attractive melody and easily comprehensible harmony. The age of the 1730s was not the age of counterpoint but of simple textures. Seen against this, Bach is out of date, provincial and *fuori moda*. Scheibe is quite right: Bach did expect his performers to cope with melody derived from the skill of his own fingers. He did write out his own embellishments – embellishments more in the tradition of old fashioned 'divisions' than the modern French ornaments. He did write textures of great polyphonic intricacy and it is often impossible to disentangle his melody by ear (though on paper all seems clear). With hindsight, we can see that Scheibe was wrong over one thing: he evokes nature as the arbiter. Bach's complexity is, to him, unnatural: but all complex art music is, from this standpoint, unnatural – and the music of the next historical phase was no less so.

Yet, this notice, which might have been shrugged off by a composer of world fame and success, probably brought home to Bach how far away he was from his time. It is one thing to curse the congregation of St Thomas's and the Leipzig Town Council for this lack of understanding, and quite another to ignore a sagacious critic, known to be at least somewhat musical, especially when he recognises your talent as a performer. One cannot help thinking that Bach was quite deeply affected by this article. Perhaps he even felt old. This growing away from the public is, of course, not a rarity for composers. In our own day, a change of management of the BBC left a myriad of middle-aged composers complaining that they were ignored in face of those frightful moderns, Schoenberg, Webern and the like, imported from the Continent. And understandably, while the great old men did not bat an eyelid, it was the less successful who felt old and unwanted. A few changed their spots, more gradually faded away.

Bach seems to have faded away. There are masterpieces to come in the last dozen years of his life, but they were, as it were, 'private masterpieces', not meant for public occasions. Only a handful of cantatas survive, and the rare ceremonial piece seems to have been a resurrection of earlier music rather than original. And certainly there is no attempt to adapt to the new favoured manner. After a career when new ideas from all over the place have been accepted into his own work, he now shuts the windows. Not that he was not interested in other men's music. There are signs that he still had an interest in the old masters, and he made a 'parody' of the religious composition now sweeping Europe, Pergolesi's *Stabat Mater*, typically adding his own contrapuntal complexities. But the readiness to see how, say, Vivaldi could be translated into German terms, or French overtures could be made a little more interesting contrapuntally, this has gone.

Bach was now more interested in tidying up his *oeuvre*. The first task seems to have been the completion of a sister volume for the *Wohltemperirte Clavier*. This was a curious thing to do. As we have seen, back in 1722, to make a public demonstration of a new system of tuning was to extend something of a tradition. One might have expected it to be published in the hope of drawing attention to it; but in fact it had not been, nor had Bach himself thought to include it in the series of volumes which he had been publishing himself under the title *Clavier-Übung* (a title borrowed from his predecessor at Leipzig, Kuhnau). He had published his partitas as the first volume of this collection in 1731 and followed it in 1735 with a book showing different styles – a 'Concerto in the Italian style' (this was the time when he was providing a repertoire for the Collegium Musicum, and this work for harpsichord without orchestra shows the style at its clearest) and an Overture, an equally French piece. But he did not publish his set of twenty-four Preludes and Fugues, nor, in the event, did he publish his second set of the same, although either would have been a worthy volume in any sense of the words *Clavier-Übung*, for superb exercises in both composition and playing they are, as well as an 'exercise' in the new method of tuning. Anyway, he began composing the pieces of this new book around 1736 and in two years had made some progress. By 1740 the collection was well on its way to completion, although transpositions of pieces to make the whole neat and tidy took more time, until, it seems in 1742 a manuscript was completed bearing the title

XXIV

Preludien und Fugen

Durch alle Ton Arten

sowohl mit der kleinen als grossen Terz

verfertiget

von

Johann Sebastian Bach

zweiter Theil: Anno 1742

Again it looks too much like a title page of a publication to allow one to think of this as a private effort; yet that it was. Bach was tidying up.

He did publish as the final part of the *Clavier-Übung* his next compilation, a set of thirty variations on a theme, today known as the *Goldberg Variations* after the player for whom they were supposedly written. One can see this as another effort at completeness, since if concertos were Italian and overtures French, variations were either English or German; though whether Bach really intended this is open to question, since it was a genre by no means exclusive to North Europeans, though practised more thoroughly and expertly by them. Still, these thirty variations are extraordinary by any standards. Firstly they are written for a two manual harpsichord – and music was rarely composed specifically with such an instrument in mind. Secondly, they are virtuoso music indeed; few players could have attempted them, although it must be said that even for the non-virtuoso they are fascinating to practise. Then, they are written on a theme which seems hardly appropriate for variations. We have already met it as a short piece in one of Anna Magdalena's commonplace books, written or copied in the 1720s. There, it was a highly ornamented (Scheibe indeed could have had a field day with it) sarabande or some such dance, leaving nothing unembellished, rather than the plain melody which most variation writers start with. But the attraction is not the tune, but the bass which provides a familiar sequence of chords on which to build, so simple that it can harmonise almost everything, so clear that even the most far-ranging fantasy will seem firmly anchored. Which is probably why Bach needs it. For he does what Beethoven in his *Diabelli Variations* and Brahms in his *Handel Variations* (both on much simpler themes than Bach's) were to do: he writes a series of pieces of different moods and character which obviously take off from the tune – and sometimes finish far away. The most extreme example is the sixteenth variation which Bach composed as a French overture, full of pompous dotted rhythms and sonorous chords. Nothing could really be farther from the finicky tune with which he had started. He writes a little fugue as the tenth variation; and finishes with a quodlibet, or set of folk tunes played simultaneously as they might be sung at a student party. Yet just to show that this is not a group of loosely connected pieces, Bach organises the whole variation set very firmly, so that every third piece is a canon, and every canon makes the melodic line be imitated at a different interval of the scale. We shall investigate this concept later, since it becomes almost obsessional with Bach in his old age. Here it may be said that it is a compositional feat of an extraordinary kind and which seems totally at odds with the idea behind the *Goldberg Variations* which seem anything but 'learned'. Yet in fact one has only to compare this work with Handel's *Chaconne in G* with sixty-two variations (written around 1732) a nice, obvious and extrovert piece just applying ordinary methods of 'division' and variation to the theme, to realise that Bach is rarely 'unlearned', rarely capable of plainness. Technical analysis does the *Goldberg Variations* rough justice; for in the end, the amazement comes from the emotional variety, the sheer overpowering satisfaction of everything in life being in order. Some variations are pretty, more are vigorous, most are intellectually taxing to follow; but in the end, comes the quodlibet – student songs – and the repeat of the theme after its considerable vicissitudes. To hear a good public performance must be a high point in anyone's life since the tension is cumulative. Yet the domestic harpsichordist – or even pianist, since the double manual is not always necessary – can reap a rich reward by attempting each piece in turn, striving to make fingers and mind obey the quirks of Bach's imagination.

The *Goldberg Variations* is the last substantial purely musical work in Bach's *oeuvre*, by which is meant that however 'learned' it in fact is, learning is not its *raison d'être*: it is not didactic. There were to be a few secular cantatas, but nothing on any grand scale. His Leipzig duties were fulfilled by repeating his earlier cantatas, quite often revising them, and he also performed, especially for Passiontide, works by others. Sometime after the *Goldberg Variations* he returned to his High Mass. He composed a setting of the Nicene Creed. Again the motive is obscure: he can have had little use for such a piece in Leipzig and he can hardly have intended to send it to Dresden to add to the *Missa*, as on an instalment plan. Nor can it have been a return to full-blooded composition, for only two sections seem to have been newly composed, the rest being reworkings of earlier music. Noticeably, performing material for the piece has not survived, and the score bears some omissions (in, for example, the figuring of the bass part) which suggest between them that performance was not the main intent. It was surely another tidying up work, perhaps on two planes: for from the autograph it is possible to see that

Bach was concerned to produce a symmetrical piece, Chorus a cappella – Tutti – Duet – Chorus – Chorus (Crucifixus) – Chorus, Aria – Chorus a cappella – Tutti (he had to make alterations in his first concept to arrive at this); while there is so much symbolism in the musical detail that it is easy to think that it is a personal statement of belief. As in the *Missa*, the manner is that of a sectional 'Neapolitan' Mass, although nothing on this scale is known in Italy. It is both long and weighty, for the chorus is employed much more than the soloists, and in a variety of styles. The two a cappella sections, the 'Credo' and the 'Confitebor', are both written in a dense contrapuntal manner, too modern harmonically to be thought of as 'old fashioned'; the 'Et resurrexit' is for a brilliant five-part choir with orchestra including trumpets (the sonority is not very different from that of the Christmas *Magnificat* of 1723); the 'Et incarnatus' is simpler but made very significant by orchestral figuration which some observers maintain includes an emblem of the Cross, while the 'Crucifixus', taken from the cantata *Weinen, Klagen* composed nearly thirty years earlier at Weimar, is a lament over a chromatic bass, as used in dramatic music for the last century. To have the words 'Et in unum Dominum' set as a duet may seem strange, but the vocal parts are canonic, illustrating that God is at least Two-in-One. Some may find the 'Credo' less satisfying than the settings by Byrd or Palestrina, or Haydn, since these composers unify the whole to give a sense of a belief in a total order in the universe. Bach's is fragmented, expressing convictions apparently not welded together; but he had still not finished with the Mass and we must reserve judgement until later.

The 'Credo' was probably put together in about 1743 and we have to wait for two more years before there is evidence of new work on the stocks. We need not assume Bach was lazy or even running out of ideas. He was approaching sixty, and at that age just the weekly round at St Thomas's must have been exhausting. He was also a distinguished man in the organ world, invited to test new organs, recommend pupils for jobs and the like, so that he was out of Leipzig fairly frequently.

As for ideas, he was less running short of them, rather that their nature was changing. We have already seen that the formal anchor of the *Goldberg Variations* was that every third number is a canon. A recent discovery shows that on Bach's own copy of them, he has added a series of fourteen more canons on the bass, obviously not to be played as part of the work, but just a composer's whim, to see how far he can go. Canon indeed had become, if not an obsession, at least a primary interest in his life and this shows a good deal about his cast of mind.

It is no coincidence that perhaps the most succinct explanation of canon is by a mathematician, Douglas Hofstadter, in whose book *Gödel, Escher, Bach: an Eternal Golden Braid*, he describes the technique thus:

The idea of a canon is that one single theme is played against itself. This is done by having 'copies' of the theme played by the various participating voices. But there are many ways to do this. The most straightforward of all canons is the round, such as 'Three Blind Mice', 'Row, Row, Row Your Boat', or 'Frère Jacques'. Here, the theme enters in the first voice and after a fixed time-delay, a 'copy' of it enters, in precisely the same key. After the same fixed time-delay in the second voice, the third voice enters carrying the theme, and so on. Most themes will not harmonise with themselves in this way. In order for a theme to work as a canon theme, each of its notes must be able to serve in a dual (or triple, or quadruple) role: it must firstly be part of a melody, and secondly it must be part of a harmonisation of the same melody. When there are three canonical voices, for instance, each note of the theme must act in two distinct harmonic ways, as well as melodically. Thus, each note in a canon has more than one musical meaning; the listener's ear and brain automatically figure out the appropriate meaning, by referring to context.

As a background to this explanation must be added that canon presupposes a set of harmonic rules also. There are consonances and dissonances, and the latter may be used only in certain circumstances. One must obey the usual ways of modulating from one key to another. These rules are generally slightly old fashioned, so that they are well defined, and the distinction between right and wrong is clear (notice that this is a distinction that few would care to make in 'practical' music). Moreover, although canon may be free, and alterations between the theme and its consequence may be made, this is considered in 'pure' canon as fair as cheating in a game of patience. Indeed in the purest canons of all, the composer will give just a single melodic line, together with a series of (often cryptic) instructions how to find its consequences. As Hofstadter puts it: 'Notice that every type of "copy" preserves all the information in the original theme, in the sense that the theme is fully recoverable from any of the copies. Such an information-preserving transformation is often called *isomorphism*, and we will have much traffic with isomorphisms in this book.' The joy, to a particular kind of mind, is that one can set oneself puzzles of differing kinds and different degrees of difficulty. It is not too hard to write a canon at the fifth (i.e. where the melody and its consequent are five notes apart) because the keys, say of C and G, have many notes and chords in common. A canon at the seventh is a very different matter. Or one can try writing a melody whose consequent will fit upside down (called 'in inversion'); or one where the consequent moves at half the speed of the melody. To the ordinary musician, these are genuine feats of skill, especially if the result sounds 'musical', that is reasonably near a consistent musical idiom.

What kind of mind becomes absorbed by such problems?

Clearly it is to some extent mathematical. It is perhaps akin to that of a chess player, for the ability to think ahead is essential in solving some of the most remote difficulties. It should be said that in spite of the usual shibboleths, it need not be particularly musical, at least in the modern world (the myth of music and mathematics being akin probably comes from Ancient Greece, where the meaning of music was a very different matter). Of the great composers, only Bach possessed it in any real measure: for Beethoven, Mozart and the rest, canon, indeed any intricate polyphony, was a peripheral skill, which, when they had to adopt it, needed extensive sketching. That Bach was fascinated with puzzles is evident, for from about 1745 onwards it was almost his sole compositorial activity. The 'Goldberg' canons are all 'perpetual', that is they can be repeated *ad libitum*. They include pieces which are in effect, several canons going on simultaneously, retrograde canons (in which, in the consequent, the melody is given backwards while the original goes forward), and canons using augmentation or diminution (the consequent part being in notes of twice or half the length of the original, respectively). He was obviously pleased with the canons for when he came to have his portrait painted in 1746 by Elias Gottlob Haussmann, he chose to be seen holding the six-part canon from this series, the only sign that he was a musician (otherwise he appears a comfortably off if slightly severe burgher) in this, the only really authentic portrait of him.

His next venture in this line was begun about 1745 and was to remain unfinished at his death, when Carl Philipp Emanuel seems to have arranged for its engraving and perhaps its title, *The Art of Fugue*. That this was not intended for practical performance is shown by the notation, the individual melodies being written out in 'old' clefs; and in any case, they are not particularly adapted to any instruments, though attempts at arrangement for keyboard(s) have been made. But clearly the aim is partly to instruct, partly to codify and solve puzzles. Thus Bach takes a single theme which he subjects to various modifications. We do not know the order of the fugues that he would have arranged, but it is not difficult to see that they could be introduced to the pupil on an easier-to-complex plan. There are canons in the volume also, one of which works on what Parry happily calls the 'hare and tortoise' basis, for by half way through, the upper part is miles ahead of the lower, which has been restricted to an inverted version of the melody in notes of double length; whereupon Bach decides to reverse the procedure so that they get home together (with a little coda to aid the conclusion of the race).

Such demonstration of skills must also have endeared him to one of the Leipzig intellectuals, Lorenz Mizler, who had founded a 'society for the musical sciences' in 1738 and recruited Bach in 1747, Bach offering a *Canon triplex a 6* as his composition on entry (this means that there are three canons given simultaneously, each working by inversion A–V; B–Я; C–Ɔ). It must be said that canons of this kind, with three melodies given and few clues on when the consequent voice is to enter, at what pitch and with what relationship (inversion, augmentation, etc.), are really in the order of crossword puzzles; and often they are capable of several solutions, some clearly better than others. For the same society he wrote five canonic variations on the Christmas hymn, *Von Himmel hoch da komm ich her*. This is more 'practical' music, written for organ, although still interested in polyphonic devices, showing how the hymn tune can be used in various canonic ways, the last variation being an astonishing affair, by which the tune is presented in canon by inversion, first at the sixth, then the third, next the second, then the ninth, finally taking to a flurry of 'diminished' canons.

And it was a practical occasion that sparked off the best

known of these displays of counterpoint. Bach's first serious biographer, Forkel's account of it is too good to miss:

His second son, Charles Philip Emanuel, entered the service of Frederick the Great in 1740. The reputation of the all-surpassing skill of John Sebastian was at this time so extended that the King often heard it mentioned and praised. This made him curious to hear and meet so great an artist. At first he distantly hinted to the son his wish that his father would one day come to Potsdam. But by degrees he began to ask him directly why his father did not come. The son could not avoid acquainting his father with these expressions of the King's; at first, however, he could not pay any attention to them because he was generally too much overwhelmed with business. But the King's expressions being repeated in several of his son's letters, he at length, in 1747, prepared to take this journey, in company of his eldest son, William Friedmann. At this time the King used to have every evening a private concert, in which he himself generally performed some concertos on the flute. One evening, just as he was getting his flute ready and his musicians were assembled, an officer brought him the written list of the strangers who had arrived. With his flute in his hand, he ran over the list, but immediately turned to the assembled musicians and said, with a kind of agitation: 'Gentlemen, old Bach is come'. The flute was now laid aside; and old Bach, who had alighted at his son's lodgings, was immediately summoned to the Palace. William Friedmann, who accompanied his father, told me this story, and I must say that I still think with pleasure on the manner in which he related it.

'Old Bach' subsequently showed his powers of improvisation, taking a subject given him by the King and making up a fugue, then, being requested for an improvised fugue in six parts, taking his own subject (since the King's might not work out) he improvised yet another fugue. When he returned to Leipzig, he decided to rewrite his improvisations and to publish them. Thus came into existence the *Musical Offering to His Royal Majesty in Prussia*, to quote the title page, in which Bach's dedication explains that he had 'noticed that, for lack of necessary preparation, the execution of the task did not fare as well as such an excellent theme [that given him by Frederick] demanded. I resolved therefore and properly pledged myself to work out this right Royal theme more fully and then make it known to the world.' Bach had a hundred copies printed, giving most away, selling the others at a thaler each. Whether (as was the eighteenth-century way) he expected, or received, a Royal reward, we do not know; but Bach's effort certainly deserved it a great deal more than most offerings to royalty.

Beginning thus, as a reminiscence of a pleasant and distinguished occasion, the *Musical Offering* is not the purely abstract collection that the *Art of Fugue* and the manuscript canons of the *Goldberg Variations* were. It contains indeed a work very much designed for performance, a trio sonata after the Italian manner; while the canons and fugues might well also be performed. Nevertheless, neither its overall design nor its contents are free from that sense of order and pedagogy that marks 'old Bach's' final years. The grand pattern has been argued recently to follow the rules of rhetoric after the precepts of Quintilian, with the two ricercars or fugues one at the beginning, the other half way through, acting as dual exordia; and given Bach's passion for rules at this time, it is a quite tenable theory. Of the individual pieces, the ricercars seem to be deliberately 'unlearned', including episodic material – which may derive from the conception of improvisation, since all improvisers have 'free' material to introduce when they run into difficulties developing the set theme. The canons are as ingenious as ever, one indeed contriving to end in the key starting a note above the original and repeating six times until it arrives at its home base an octave above – Bach writing 'as the key rises, so may the King's Glory'.

These abstract works of Bach's old age have puzzled

musicians and scholars. Parry, as sympathetic and under-standing a commentator on Bach as could be, goes into elaborate excuses about the quality of the *Musical Offering*, pointing out that improvised music is never as successful as carefully penned music, and argues that the trio sonata is not as good as others since to work out the 'King's' theme cannot produce music attaining 'the highest level of interest'. Indeed, Parry seems to think that in the *Art of Fugue* Bach has succumbed to the temptation to demonstrate his skill, although why this should be described as a 'temptation' is not clear. But seen both personally and historically, it is not so great a surprise to find Bach taking to such pursuits.

Personally, the blood runs colder in most men as they grow older; but, at least before senility sets in, they frequently have not only minds packed with experience but the energy to use it. In many composers, their later work has somewhat less warmth and achieves a remoter quality. This can be seen in the last period of Beethoven's life; and also Mozart's, as a comparison of the warmth of the characters in *The Marriage of Figaro* and the beautifully ordered but more puppet-like personages of *Così fan tutte* of Mozart's final months show; and these are two of many.

Historically, the purpose usually ascribed to music, the expression of human emotion, is largely a creation of the Renaissance. It was in the humanist courts of northern Italy that the theory was born of an artwork – combining music and words in such as way as to create a 'third' force – which would 'muovere gli affetti', a phrase which might be translated as 'to move the whole man'. As we have seen, it was only after it had proved capable of codification in the 'theory of the affections' that it caught on in Germany. But Germany never underwent the thorough inculcation of humanist ideas as did Italy. We must remember that before the Renaissance, the idea of music as patterns in sound was quite common. The

Netherlands composers of the later fifteenth century were as intrigued with canons as polyphonic device as Bach was; as were the writers of 'chases' or 'caccie' in the movement we know as the 'Ars Nova'. Bach indeed is in many ways a medieval composer, and could have only developed thus in a Germany which had largely passed directly from the Gothic to the Baroque, and in a profession in which the direct expression of human emotion (as in opera) is not a primary interest. This is no reason for us to ascribe this love of a 'numbered' music to some form of search for God's 'truth': after all, the perpetual canon of the *Musical Offering* was written to the glory of Frederick the Great. It is one of man's legitimate interests that we, living in the post-Webern age, should not find hard to acknowledge. Music can provide many pleasures, some physical (some musicians love arriving at the perfection of co-ordination in playing scales or achieving the sweetness of sound of bow on strings), some social (joining together in chamber music, or singing in choirs), some emotional, some intellectual. And rather than attempt a hierarchy, it is perhaps better to accept the truth: 'in my Father's house, are many mansions'.

In a way it is more of a puzzle to find Bach, still in 1748, writing away again at his 'High Mass'. The *Missa* for Dresden of 1733 has surely turned into some form of symbol of completeness. The 'Creed' has been finished. He now adds the 'Sanctus' which must have startled the congregation at St Thomas's on Christmas Day 1724; to which he appended as 'Osanna', an arrangement of a chorus from the serenata *Preise dein Glücke* written for the Elector August III in 1734. The 'Benedictus' is a tenor aria in the usual cantata style, with obbligato flute, and may also be a reworking of earlier music. The 'Agnus Dei' is another aria, for contralto, written originally as 'Ach bleibe doch, mein liebstes Leben' in the Ascension Day Oratorio in 1735. Finally for the 'Dona nobis pacem' he takes the *stile antico* chorus already used for the 'Gratias agimus tibi' in the 'Gloria' and just changes the words. It was a procedure quite common in church music at this time, especially in the doxologies of psalms or Magnificat, where the text 'Sicut erat in principio' acts as an open invitation.

What a ragbag! And this from a man who had spent the last few years working out all the possibilities of this theme or that concept! It is also an impractical ragbag. The assembled Mass in this form is too long to be even thought of in terms of church ceremonial (whereas the *Missa* of two movements could well have been included in the *Hauptgottesdienst* at Leipzig). Equally, the resources demanded lack the sense of practical music making. The choir is now divided into four, now in five, once in eight. The number of movements it is expected to sing make the piece so tiring that when the grandeur of the 'Sanctus' comes, the singers are often too exhausted to do it justice (whereas at Christmas 1724 it would have been meat to a choir relatively fresh). The soloists are not used with any consistency either, and certainly their parts show no signs of being designed for any particular group or individuals. The orchestra is treated equally summarily. Quite apart from the grotesque 'Quoniam' with its difficult horn solo given to a player who has had no chance to warm up, the trumpet parts are sporadic and taxing while the woodwind players are kept busy. No doubt it was a more logical orchestration for the eighteenth century, when players were expected to change instruments constantly, but even then it would have posed difficulties. The work is a nightmare to any analyst, from whatever point of view he approaches it, who feels that there should be some essential unity in a masterpiece. For a masterpiece it certainly is, as will be agreed by any performer who has taken part in a carefully prepared performance, and by any listener who is at home with Baroque music. The 'Kyrie' is, for singers or players or listeners, an embarkation on a great adventure and the homecoming as the trumpets soar in the 'Dona nobis pacem' is one of the most satisfying experiences not just in music but in life.

Bach seem to have been a healthy man. There are occasional documents which show that Anna Magdalena was sometimes ill, and it would be remarkable if, with twenty children, there were not infections around the family from time to time. Yet there is no document, such as one finds with many composers in constant employment, which reports the necessity for a deputy or a leave of absence, or the cancellation of a recital. The portrait of 1746 shows a sturdy man. About that time, however, his eyes began to trouble him, and by the beginning of 1749 a serious cataract had developed. His state was such that the Town Council began to look round for his successor – which was done clumsily, though such committees have their duties to see that posts are speedily filled and that interregnums are kept to a minimum. But 'old Bach' was not finished with. The Rector of a school in Freiburg had been denigrating the necessity for music in the curriculum and Bach came out apparently as vigorously as ever to support his colleague, the *Kantor*. But the blindness became so bad that Bach decided to have an operation by one of the foremost eye surgeons of the age, the Englishman John Taylor, who was eventually to do a similar service for Handel. Alas, it did not succeed and a second attempt in April 1750 weakened Bach considerably. He took his final communion at his house in July and died on the twenty-eighth of the month after a stroke.

The world went on. The Town Council appointed the man they had considered before Bach's death, the member for Defence, as already noted, declaring that they wanted a *Kantor* not a *Kapellmeister*. One hopes that Cantor Harrer, who took up his duties on 29 September (Michaelmas), 'understood music'! Anna Magdalena petitioned for 'half a year's grace' to the Town Council and asked them to appoint a guardian for the five children still in her care (among them Johann Christian). By October, she had decided not to marry again and appointed Bach's old colleague, Görner, as her co-guardian.

Bach's estate shows a list of possessions such as one might expect of a burgher. There was not a great deal of money; there were the furnishings of a comfortable home; there was a considerable number of instruments including seven harpsichords and a valuable violin by Stainer; there was a miniature library, mainly theology. In no wise was it enough to keep Anna Magdalena in comfort, but in any case it had to be divided between her and the nine surviving children of the two marriages. The manuscripts of the music were divided between Anna Magdalena, Carl Philipp Emanuel and Wilhelm Friedmann. Those possessed by Anna were given by her to the Thomasschule. Carl Philipp Emanuel kept his and eventually they were deposited in the Royal Library in Berlin. Wilhelm Friedmann, often in financial straits, sold his share piecemeal, to the despair of later scholars; though it must be said that in an age which scarcely recognised the music of the recent past, he can have had no idea of their ultimate value.

In 1754, Mizler published in his *Musikalische Bibliothek* an obituary notice written by Carl Philipp Emanuel and Johann Friedrich Agricola. They produced an accurate outline of his career, adding a number of details that would otherwise never have come down to us, including a list of his principal works whch allowed scholars to look for the right things when his music came to be published in the nineteenth century. It is an affectionate portrait, of an energetic, likeable man and stupendous musician. He had a fine ear and 'in conducting he was very accurate, and of the tempo, which he generally took very lively, he was uncommonly sure'. He was serious but not without a sense of humour and he was the most upright of men 'towards God and his neighbour'. Few men, and certainly few musicians, can have come off so well in the eyes of a son-musician.

4 The legacy

So Bach died; but we cannot leave him there. For one thing, the dynasty went on, and for another, the legend grew. Of his twenty children, ten survived beyond infancy and five of them became professional musicians. This might be thought to confirm the stern picture of the master forcing the next generation to follow the family tradition. Yet the more we know of the Bach sons, the more their father seems to have been that most favoured of teachers, one who finds his pupils branching off into new ways. The nearest of them to him in temperament was Carl Philipp Emanuel, a serious musician who spent years at the Potsdam court of Frederick the Great before himself becoming a *Kantor* at Hamburg. Like his father, he was something of a pedagogue and wrote the standard eighteenth-century work on keyboard playing, the *Versuch über die wahre Art das Clavier zu spielen*, published first in 1753 and reissued several times before the end of the century. He was a fluent composer (the standard list of his works approaches nine hundred separate items), and also one of broad tastes: for although in the manner of his father he never pursued merely fashionable ways, he was not averse to writing music in an up-to-date style and certainly he was concerned to please his masters, whether kings at Potsdam or the church elders at Hamburg.

But Carl Philipp Emanuel was not *the* Bach: that title must be accorded his younger brother Johann Christian, with whom the family name became synonymous from the 1770s. Already in his teens he had gone to Italy to study and imbibe the style of Italian opera; and in his early twenties he became a Roman Catholic. Thereafter he gradually became one of the best known composers of his day, active in London, much admired by Mozart, and wildly prosperous for a time, although owing some £4,000 at his death in 1782. If this son's conversion to the alien faith would surely have come as a shock to his father, one suspects that J. S. B. would have liked his elder son, Wilhelm Friedmann's career even less. He had been the old man's favourite son, did all the right things such as studying, with success, at Leipzig University, becoming organist at the Dresden Sophienkirche, where he mixed in such high flown musical circles as those of Hasse and his wife Faustina, and then moving on to Halle where the Liebfrauen-kirche received him as organist without even the usual test. But the authorities found him a difficult man, he seems to have missed the chance to be *Kapellmeister* at the Darmstadt court simply owing to his lack of tact. Gradually life went downhill and he too died poor.

This was the last generation of the dynasty to make any real mark on the musical profession. Certainly there was a grand-child of the old man who made a decent living in music – and in Berlin too. But when Wilhelm Friedrich Ernst died in 1845, the Bachs had really disappeared from the stage. Or rather, from the current scene: but a revival had taken place. Wilhelm Friedrich Ernst had attended the unveiling of a monument to his grandfather at Leipzig in 1843. By that time the legend was already strong. In fact the same chain of cir-cumstances which was responsible for the demise of the Bach musical clan also led to the rise of the Bach legend. The French Revolution, with its recasting of society, changed central Europe radically. From the more than three hundred small states with their *Kapellmeistern* and *Kapellen* only thirty-nine emerged as the German Confederation in 1815. Gone were the jobs for efficient if scarcely charismatic com-posers and performers; and the famous free cities which had had their musical lives overseen by the great *Kantors* were equally diminished in importance. But in place of the plethora of little states, Germany was now almost in existence, lacking the confidence of even a defeated France, and looking for roots. It was a Germany led from Berlin; where Carl Philipp Emanuel had worked until nearly 1770 and whose substantial collection of his father's manuscripts eventually came into the possession of the state library; where history rather than archaeology was now becoming a serious study, the documents of Rome replacing the monuments of Greece in their fascination for scholars.

These interests and opportunities combined to give rise to a kind of Bach revival as early as the 1780s. At first it was a rather narrow circle of aficionados who took to the Bach cult. Of these *Kennern*, it was the former Austrian Ambassador to Berlin who, back in Vienna, showed his musical finds to Haydn and to Mozart; the latter must have been among the first to use a Bach technique as a religious symbol, when, in *The Magic Flute*, he wrote a full scale chorale prelude as a duet for the mysterious but undoubtedly Godly Armed Men. But such musicians, brought up in the age of delicious melody and simple harmony were mainly fascinated by the great polyphony of the fugues, the endless skills in canon and contrapuntal device. Those who were gifted enough could learn much from the supreme pedagogue: so did Mozart, the finale to whose *Jupiter Symphony* is inconceivable without his knowledge of Bach; so did Haydn and later, Beethoven, who was put to study the *Forty-eight* at an early age. It must be said that none of these really understood the basis of Bach's music, and they knew very little of the cantatas and *Passions*, or even the *B minor Mass* (some scholars' view that the *Missa Solemnis* is its direct descendant lacks supporting evidence).

It was only to a subsequent generation that Bach was the composer rather than the teacher. Carl Friedrich Zelter, who was conductor of the Berlin Singakademie, one of the earliest of the middle-class, non-professional choirs (and hence the ancestor of all the Bach Choirs throughout the world), was a confirmed musical antiquarian. He had inherited some Bach scores and he performed some of the motets (easier to understand and to provide forces for than the cantatas). He thought the Passions and the *B minor Mass* were too difficult, but he allowed his bright, twenty-year-old pupil, Mendelssohn to rehearse and then perform the *St Matthew Passion* in 1829. No doubt today we would be horrified at what the audience heard. There were cuts and alterations, the instrumentation was changed (who in 1829 had ever heard an *oboe d'amore?*) and the style was clearly highly romantic. But this was exactly the need of the moment. After all, was not Bach really a Romantic? Had not Scheibe said that Bach's 'onerous labour and uncommon effort' were 'vainly employed, since they conflict with nature'? At last he was seen as a real composer, expressing the richness of human emotion and therefore worthy of revival.

And revived he was. Already he had acquired a proselytizer of power in Johann Nicolaus Forkel, whose extended essay *On Johann Sebastian Bach's Life, Genius, and Works* had come out in 1802 and had been published in an English translation in 1820. There Bach appears as not only a great composer but a paragon of a father, and an agreeable colleague, who loved nothing better than to play the viola, that most unassuming instrument, at musical parties. Forkel ends significantly: 'And this man, the greatest musical poet and the greatest musical orator that ever existed, and probably ever will exist, was a German. Let his country be proud of him; let it be proud, but, at the same time, worthy of him!' Naturally Bach was taken up by what might be called (a little unkindly) the Biedermeier group, the composers of and for that middle class which sang in Zelter's Singverein and its imitators. Bach's attitude 'Anyone who works as hard as I did will get as far' appealed to the bourgeoisie of the Protestant Work Ethic. Probably the most deeply affected of this group was, as might be expected, Mendelssohn. Not only did he write organ fugues, but the whole concept of music as a moral force, seen so strongly in the choral works, must eventually be traced back to Bach. Schumann, who took to the pedal piano – an ordinary piano with a pedal board after the manner of the organ – instructed the boys and girls for whom his *Album for the Young* was planned, to practise Bach assiduously. Brahms hardly belongs to this group simply because Bach was only one of the many Baroque composers whose music he knew well. But it must surely have been Bach who inspired him to write so grand a fugue to cap his *Variations on a Theme of Handel*. *Echt* Protestant though he was, Bach was not unknown to the Roman Catholics, Bruckner copying out the *Art of Fugue* in the 1840s; while Liszt had a period of transcribing and arranging mainly the organ works from about 1855 (his fine transcription of the great *G minor Fantasia and Fugue* dates from 1863). In 1855 he also wrote his tremendous Fugue on BACH; and the use of the anagram would surely have pleased Johann Sebastian Bach, as probably would have the huge virtuosity involved in playing the piece.

No doubt some of this vogue was due to German nationalism asserting itself at a time when some of the principal musical posts still went to foreigners. No doubt also that in a time which was exploring the past (as exemplified in Leopold von Ranke's *History of the Popes*) Bach provided a focal point for the musicians. But more than that, for such composers as Schumann, Bach and his fugues were worth emulation for their strict discipline. If we look at Schumann's early piano music, beautiful though much of it is, it is undeniably self indulgent, following the inspiration of the moment and the fingers without real consistency of texture or sonority.

Schumann and others turned to Beethoven for models of their symphonies but these are often too large undertakings for men who were essentially miniaturists. 'The seams show' as Tchaikovsky was to say self-disparagingly. Fugue, on the other hand, is – or at least can be – a relatively small genre, if you can master its polyphonic ways. It does not require or even encourage over-inflation. So did it fit into the Romantic style and its practitioners became better composers. The deep, religious seriousness of German nineteenth-century music was also helped by the Bachian re-discovery. When the truly popular music of Italy was the melodramas of Verdi, that of Paris the extravagances of Meyerbeer at the Opéra, Wagner could think of High Art. It is no coincidence that by the time his Hans Sachs was singing near the end of *The Mastersingers of Nuremberg*

> Honour your German masters
> If you would shun disasters

in the 1860s, Bach indeed was honoured: a great collected edition of his works had been started with the publication of the scores of ten cantatas in 1851. It was to take until 1900 to complete, but it was a magnificent undertaking and for its time, well executed, being reliable and based on original scores in a way that many 'historical' editions were not. About two hundred books were written about him in the nineteenth century, a very large number for that epoch, including a standard biography, Spitta's *Johann Sebastian Bach* (1873–1880), which became a model of its kind since it put Bach firmly against the background of German Lutheran music of the Baroque while establishing many details about his life. Most of this literature was in German but a surprising amount of it (including Spitta) was translated into English soon after publication; and a proliferation of Bach societies and choirs had begun.

So had arrived a paradoxical change. From the interest in Bach as a supreme craftsman from such devout Roman Catholics as Haydn and Mozart, he now became the symbol of 'Teutonic religion', to quote the Anglican Parry's unhappy phrase. Parry indeed was a fairer and more far-seeing scholar than most. He recognised the Italianate features in Bach's works and saw that his real gift was for painting human situations (his comments on the *St Matthew Passion* are a model of good sense in this respect). Nevertheless, it was Bach the devout that dominated both performers and writers at the 150 year mark after J. S. B's death. The high priest of this point of view was Albert Schweitzer, whose study came out in 1905, who worked out the symbolism inherent in all Bach's music, finding a quite concrete imagery in each motif and phrase. By such an interpretation, Schweitzer can interpret the mind of the composer, who becomes a mystic capable of ecstasy; his skill is 'no longer simply a technique, but an interpretation of the world, an image of Being'; and 'his music is a phenomenon of the reality of the inconceivable as is the cosmos itself'.

This kind of adulation and interpretation virtually came to an end with the First World War, although it has adherents to this day. After a spate of books in the first decade of the century, there were comparatively few for many years. In Germany, the disasters first of war, then of economics and finally of politics were scarcely fruitful ground for the reappraisal of a solid Lutheran – though the music continued to be performed by the middle-class choral societies of northern Europe. The scholars must have thought that Spitta had said something like the final word. But the subject was too attractive, the problems too many for them to set Bach aside, and if only one great scholar, Arnold Schering, worked away diligently to produce his masterpiece *A Musical History of Leipzig in the Age of Bach and Hiller* published in 1941 at the very end of his life, there was always a steady stream of articles for the *Bach Yearbook*, now tackling problems of authenticity of this or that piece, or of this or that portrait (Bach iconography has always found itself in difficulties), or how one is to interpret his notation correctly. But except for the organists and the choral directors, Bach was of less interest than he had been. The intellectuals such as Ezra Pound took to Vivaldi; the musicians such as Stravinsky took to Pergolesi, an equally implausible *Kleinmeister*. When the Jewish scholars were driven from Germany, Bach had few protectors even there. This author can still remember the heavy-footed performances, Sir Henry Wood battling through the *Third Brandenburg Concerto* with a hundred or more strings, or the placing of a similar piece at the beginning of a concert, paying appropriate homage before settling down to the pleasures of the evening. Bach had once again retreated to the study.

At the end of the Second World War, Germany seemed an even less appropriate place to think of reviving the reputation of its Protestant religious composer. Indeed, its principal heir to Spitta and Schering, Friedrich Blume, wrote gloomily in 1947 that the time would have been ripe for the production of an entirely new edition of Bach's complete works if the distress and impoverishment of the times and the loss of very many of the sources had not withdrawn from the German people all prospect and possibility of such an undertaking. Which only shows that great scholars are rarely great prophets. By 1954 a *Neue Bach-Ausgabe* was on its way. The significance of this new collected edition goes far beyond its provision of new texts for the music: the old Bach edition was not at all bad in that respect. It lies in the way the work has been undertaken. An institute was set up in Göttingen and all the new science of musicology was pressed into service. Every score was assembled on film; nearly every original copyist was identified; watermarks and paper were examined; and the documents of Bach's life were given a similar treatment. This, more than any other, is the way to knowledge of a working musician. We now can date his works more accurately – sometimes very accurately indeed – find out about his working methods, where he found difficulties, which things he found easy. We can see where he made improvements – or perhaps simply alterations – when he rewrote or 'parodied' a piece later in life. This is the stuff of a composer's life. Bach may have been a mystic, an ecstatic – but that view may shed more light on Schweitzer's mentality than his subject's. He may have been a convinced Lutheran who sought his salvation in writing music and persuading others to virtue. He may be considered the last of the medieval craftsmen in music, the product of a Germany which missed the Renaissance. All this is speculation. What is not is that he was a thoroughly professional musician, doing his job day in, day out, sometimes so short of time that he had to use up formerly invented materials, sometimes in a mood for brilliant improvising, sometimes content to set himself and solve puzzles. And with these twists and turns of everyday life go the changes which come over men as their decades progress. Whereas the picture of Bach commonly held in the nineteenth century was of a monument, a Godhead obstructed by the daily task and the minnows who surrounded him at Leipzig, a man with a mission which was frustrated by those years serving mammon at Cöthen, we can now see that he was all of these things and many more. In which he is like the generality of humanity. Young men glory in their skills; great virtuosity is mainly the gift of the young. Having scaled their Everests, they have to find new targets elsewhere – which no doubt explains why Bach left the organ loft for some years. Religion is often the resource of the middle-aged, as the cocoon of immortality grows thinner and the soul needs reassurance in the world both of ideas and emotions. Finally comes that cooling of the blood in advancing years: the die is cast and what is left is the search for some kind of orderly perfection (which is perhaps why a number of composers have taken to counterpoint in their declining years – even the young but dying Mozart in 1790–1, Beethoven in the late quartets, Verdi in the final fugue of *Falstaff*). One of the missing facets of human experience in Bach is any sense of nostalgia. Bach never looks back. There has never been a Golden Age. He faces new problems to the end.

Philology has thus caused a reappraisal. And so has what might be called the cleaning of the musical portrait. For with the revival of 'original' instruments and methods of playing, we can now hear Bach's works in something like the sonorities he imagined. He was slow to benefit from this movement, firstly because his demands on the performer are such that the amateurs and quasi-amateurs who first began to try out what his music might sound like on, say, an unmodernised violin, could hardly tackle him; and secondly, because since his greatest works were so familiar a second-rate performance, albeit nearer to the sound of his choir and band in St Thomas's, seemed so dismal. Nevertheless, as time has gone on, the Bach *oeuvre* has increasingly been revived – and revealed.

The most striking change is caused simply by using the correct number of instruments and voices. The massed choirs of enthusiastic amateurs may emphasise devotion; the new professionals of the chamber choir, the going back to the boys-plus-men of the Lutheran church choir (as in so many recordings) gives a litheness, puts an emphasis on line and skill. Speeds come naturally a little faster, phrasing becomes more articulate, with more breathing spaces and less legato continuity. Similarly, orchestras are no longer based on Sir Henry Wood's dictum that 'you can never have enough strings'. With a single player (or just two or three) to a part, the strings no longer dominate but are on equal terms with oboes and flutes (or even harpsichords). Add the use of the short Baroque bow, wind instruments made of wood rather than metal, with a mechanism which cannot make all notes equally easy of speaking, and a new springiness comes into the music. Even the organ music acquires this bounce when played on the new style instruments with their tracker action which allows for immediate contact between foot, finger and pipe rather than passing through intermediate actions as in the nineteenth-century instrument. The sheer joy of Bach's virtuosity is quickly evident on such an organ.

Modern technology has also contributed. What would Bach have thought of the recordings of his cantatas, where there has been ample rehearsal time for singers and players of much better quality than he could expect at Leipzig? And where, moreover, the mistakes can be corrected at the touch of a switch, the wrong note or harshness of tone (or even the need for surpassing breath control) quickly substituted by a perfect version? Are we not, perhaps, for the first time hearing what Bach imagined in his composing room at St Thomas's and which he clearly never heard on those despairing Sundays?

This is the most radical change of view about a composer in the history of music. Friedrich Blume, who in 1947 was postulating the investigation of orthodox Lutheran thinking as the next step towards the understanding of Bach's mind, was fifteen years later pointing out that Bach was the son not of a church but a town musician; that most of his life had been spent on other things than church music; and that Telemann and Graupner had actually composed more church music than J.S.B. He points out that that was also Forkel's portrait of the composer; it was the later commentators who turned Bach into the Lutheran *Kantor*, the preacher of Bible and chorale.

So we have a new Bach. It would be arrogant to say that he is old J. S. B. himself; cleaning portraits does not in itself ensure greater understanding of their subject. Nevertheless, he appeals to more people than ever. His congregations at St Thomas's were insignificant by comparison with even the most sparsely heard broadcast; and the total membership of all the bourgeois Bach Choirs of the nineteenth century cannot compete with the number of people who buy the collected editions of the cantatas recorded by this or that German choir.

The arrival of this popularity with the new picture of Bach is not fortuitous. The portrait is much to the taste of our age. We do not much care for preachers, and orthodox Christian belief is less middle-of-the-road than it was. We like men who can solve problems and invent patterns, and are not particularly impressed by them if they have to work hard to do this (it is difficult to believe in Bach practising the organ, or writing contrapuntal exercises day by day). But above all, the old picture of Bach the seeker after death would not attract today. We demand to be cured; and Bach's liveliness, especially in the new mode of performance, does just that. He is an invigorating composer, not so much one for the beginning of a concert as for sending us home with a life-enhancing fugal finale, brightly argued to the last note. And a caring one, as the humanity of the great Passions shows. How long this portrait will last no one can say; that it is not the final one is quite certain. But at the moment it is a good one to have.

Further reading

The literature about J. S. Bach is vast, but most of it is addressed to specialists and concerns the detail of his life or music. Comprehensive surveys are comparatively rare, especially those written since World War II, with new research advancing so rapidly that scholars are afraid of being out of date. Suggestions for further reading for the non-musician are therefore not as plentiful as might be expected.

The essential book on the life in English is David and Mendel, *The Bach Reader* (London, rev. edition 1966), a translation of all the important documents, obituaries and views of Bach's contemporaries about his music. Its major deficiency is a lack of background information which is sometimes necessary for full understanding of the documents. It should therefore be supplemented by the best purely biographical work, C. S. Terry, *Bach: a Biography* (London, 1928), ageing but still reliable and always interesting in its portrayal of both man and background. The dynasty is treated in Percy Young, *The Bachs 1500–1850* (London, 1970). The best modern account of dynasty, man and music is the excellent article on the Bach family by Christoff Wolff in *The New Grove Dictionary of Music and Musicians* (London, 1980). The way the overall picture of Bach has been arrived at is discussed by Friedrich Blume in a little book translated into English as *Two Centuries of Bach* (London, 1950) and an article bringing that picture up to date is 'Outlines of a New Picture of Bach', in *Music and Letters*, XLIV (1963), pp. 214 ff.

There is no recent book in any language to provide a comprehensive study of Bach's *oeuvre*. The best way of obtaining an overall picture is probably to read the relevant chapters in a general history of eighteenth-century music, such as Manfred Bukhofzer, *Music in the Baroque Era* (New York, 1947) or the more up-to-date Claude Palisca, *Baroque Music* (Englewood Cliffs, NJ, 1968, rev. edition 1981) and *The New Oxford History of Music*, Vol. V (1975). Of the different genres, the cantatas have received the best treatment with a two-volume study, W. G. Whittaker, *The Cantatas of Johann Sebastian Bach*, the value of which is enhanced in its reprint

(London, 1978) by the inclusion of the new datings contained originally in A. Dürr, *Die Kantaten von Johann Sebastian Bach* (Kassel,
1971). A short but incisive and serviceable account of this material is
contained in J. A. Westrup, *Bach Cantatas* (London, 1966). The
remaining church music has, by comparison, received indifferent
attention. The chapters in *The New Oxford History of Music*, Vol. V,
recommended above, give the most thorough account, though
intended for the music student rather than the general public. There
is a useful short account of Passion music in B. Smallman, *The
Background of Passion Music, J. S. Bach and his Predecessors* (rev.
edition New York, 1970). Studies of the instrumental music are just
as rare. A two-volume study by Peter Williams, *The Organ Music of
J. S. Bach* (Cambridge, 1980) is meant more for the player than
the listener. The concertos are dealt with in Arthur Hutchings
The Baroque Concerto (London, 1961, rev. edition 1973) and the
orchestra which played them in C. S. Terry, *Bach's Orchestra*
(London, 1932, rev. edition 1966). An interesting discussion of
Bach's methods of work, based on an examination of manuscripts is
R. L. Marshall, *The Compositional Process of J. S. Bach* (Princeton,
1972).

After this not too happy picture, it is a pleasure to say that Bach's
music has been well treated in modern editions. The old collected
edition of the *Bach Gesellschaft* (1851–1900) was the best of the
nineteenth-century ventures of this kind and provided the material
for countless editions, sometimes called optimistically 'Urtext',
accurate and relatively unembellished by scholarly or musicianly
fantasy. The *Neue Bach Gesellschaft* edition (begun 1954) is even
better, providing an accurate text (modernised only in respects
which make it more easily comprehensible to the performer) to
which is added more than adequate critical commentary which tells
much about the work itself, its background and sources. This edition
also devotes several volumes to the documentary and visual material
about Bach's life. There is thus little excuse for anyone using
romantic interpretations of the original; and to their credit, the
gramophone companies recording the vast cantata repertoire, or
using 'authentic' instruments for the concerto collections try to
recreate the sound which Bach might have imagined – a pursuit for
the performer which will happily continue like a *canon in perpetuum*.

Index

Compiled by Elsie Arnold

Abel, C. F., 22

affections, theory of, 14 f., 44, 61, 66 ff., 93

Agricola, Johann Friedrich (pupil of Bach), 85

Albinoni (composer), 9

d'Anglebert (composer), 25

August III, Elector of Saxony, 59 ff., 63, 64, 82

Bach family: Johann Ambrosius (father of J.S.B.), 2; Carl Philipp Emanuel (son), 6, 17, 57, 65, 77, 85, 87, 89; Johann Christian (son), 85, 87 f.; Wilhelm Friedmann (son), 6, 17, 25, 57, 65, 85, 88; Wilhelm Friedrich Ernst (grandson), 88

Bach, Johann Sebastian: birth and early education of, 2 ff.; organist at Arnstadt, 3 f.; organist at Mühlhausen, 4 ff.; organist at Weimar, 6 ff.; first wife, 4, 6, death of, 34; Weimar: *Konzertmeister* at, 10 f.; musical resources at, 12; cantata composition at, 12 ff.; imprisoned at, 16; second wife, Anna Magdalena Wülken, 34, 84, 85; Leipzig: University Collegium Musicum, directorship of, 53, 55, 56, 58, 70; Town Council of, 59, 65, 69, 84; dispute with headmaster of the Thomasschule, 65; cataract and death, 84

Compositions: Anna Magdalena's commonplace books, 26, 50, 72; *The Art of Fugue*, 77 f.; Brandenburg Concertos, 19 ff.; canons, 75 ff., *Canon triplex a 6*, 78; five canonic variations on *Von Himmel hoch*, 78; cantatas, 5, 13, 15, 18, 39 ff., 50, 69; *Chaconne in D minor* arr. Busoni, 33; chorale preludes, 68; *Christmas Oratorio*, 63 f.; *Clavier-Übung*, 70 f.; concertos: in D minor for clavier, 57; for two claviers, 58; for three claviers, 57; for violin in A minor, 19, D minor, 20, E major, 19 f.; for two violins in D minor, 19 f.; *English suites*, 26; *French suites/overtures*, 23 ff., 55; *Goldberg Variations*, 50, 71 ff., 80; Magnificat, first setting of, 45, 74; *Mass in B minor*: Gloria influenced by Vivaldi, 9; *Sanctus in D major*, 46; Kyrie and Gloria sent to Elector of Saxony, 60 ff., 64, 82 ff.; *Musical Offering*, 79 ff.; Nicene Creed, 73 f.; partitas, 51; Passions: *St John*, 46, 48 f., 51; *St Matthew*, 47, 48, 51 ff.; sonatas: for violin, 30, for flute, 30 f.; Suite in B minor for flute and strings, 55; suites/sonatas for unaccompanied violin, 31 ff., unaccompanied cello, 31 ff.; two- and three-part inventions, 27; *Well-tempered clavier*, 28 f., 33, 70 f., 89

Beethoven, 72, 77, 81, 89, 92, 96

Bellini, 21

Berlin, 17, 89

Biber (composer), 31

Biedermeier group of composers, 90

Blume, Friedrich (music historian), 94, 97

Bodenschatz (anthologist of church music), 38

Böhm, Georg (organist and composer), 3

Bononcini, Giovanni (composer), 42

Brahms, 72, 91

Brockes (librettist), 47, 48

Bruckner (composer), 91

Busoni, 33

Buxtehude (organist and composer), 4, 8

Calov, Abraham (theologian), 58

Celle, 3

Chopin, 30

Corelli (violinist and composer), 8 f.

Couperin-le-Grand, François (harpsichordist and composer), 25 f.

Darmstadt, 35, 88

Dresden, 9, 17, 21, 33, 35, 60 ff., 64 f., 88

Druse (musician), 15 f.

Elgar, 47

Fischer, J. C. F. (composer), 29, 33

Forkel (biographer), 79, 90, 97

Franck, Salomo (librettist), 10, 12 f.

Frederick the Great, 31, 79 f., 82, 87

Froberger (composer), 2

Geminiani (violinist and composer), 9

Graupner (composer), 35, 41, 97

Halle, 10, 88

Hamburg, 3, 11, 34, 47, 65

Handel, 43, 47, 68

Hanover, 11

Harrer (Cantor), 84

Hasse, Johann Adolf and his wife Faustina (composer and opera singer respectively), 61, 68, 88

Haussmann, Elias Gottlob (painter), 77

Haydn, 89, 93

Heinichen (composer and writer), 67

Henrici, Christian Friedrich (Picander, librettist), 50, 52, 63

Hofstadter, Douglas (mathematician), definition of canon, 75 f.

Keiser (composer), 47

Kerll (composer), 2

Kuhnau (composer), 35, 39, 48, 70

Liszt, 91

Locatelli (violinist and composer), 9

Lübeck, 4

Lully, 23

Mattheson, Johann (composer, writer), *Der musikalische Patriot*, 34

Mendelssohn, 90, 91

Mizler, Lorenz, 78, 85

Monteverdi, 67

Mozart, 58, 77, 81, 89, 93, 96

Neue Bach-Ausgabe, 94 f.

Neumeister (librettist), 40, 44

Pachelbel (composer), 2, 29

Parry, Sir Hubert (composer and scholar), 81, 93

Pergolesi (composer), 14, 70, 94

Picander, *see* Henrici

Plato, 67

Pound, Ezra (poet), 94

Quintilian (theorist of rhetoric), 80

Ranke, Leopold von (historian), 91
Reincken (musician), 3
Roger, Etienne (music publisher), 23
Rome, 17

Scarlatti, Domenico (composer), 51
Scheibe, Johann Adolph (writer on music), 66, 68 f., 72, 90
Schering, Arnold (music historian), 93, 94
Schoenberg, 29, 69
Schumann, 91, 92
Schweitzer, Albert (organist and writer), 14, 93, 95
Shaw, G. B., 32
Silbermann (organ builder), 64
Spitta (music historian), 92 f., 94
Spork, Count von, 46
Steffani, Agostino (composer and court official), 11
Steiglitz (Burgomaster), 37
Stöltzel (composer), 50
Stravinsky, 94

Taskin (harpsichord maker), 25
Taylor, John (eye surgeon), 84
Telemann (composer), 16, 35, 36, 40, 41, 54, 97

Veracini (violinist and composer), 9, 31
Verdi, 96
Versailles, 3, 11, 14, 26, 56
Vinci (composer), 42
Vivaldi, 8 f., 18 ff., 56 f., 62, 94

Wagner, *Tristan and Isolde*, 29
Walsh (music publisher), 23, 58
Walther J. G. (organist and composer), 6, 9
Webern, 69
Whittaker, W. G. (musical scholar), 41
Wood, Sir Henry (conductor), 94, 96
word painting, *see* affections, theory of

Zelter, Carl Friedrich (conductor and musical antiquarian), 89 f.